CH00869188

Into the Light
George Lawson
with Bob Mallick

The medium is the message

George Frederick Lawson was born in Bridgeton, Glasgow on 19 May, 1956, the second son of Lena and Frank Lawson.

Acknowledging his spiritual gifts in 2007, he now works with other well-respected mediums at the Spiritualist Association of Great Britain (SAGB). He does this alongside public platform demonstrations around the world as well as a busy schedule of private readings.

George is driven by the mission to serve and bring comfort, a drive that he acknowledges as from a higher power, to which he surrenders completely and joyfully. The man and his work aim to proclaim the truth of divine love and eternal life. Some names have been changed to protect privacy..

George's tale of turbulence and misadventure, childhood neglect, youthful folly and adult self-indulgence, with all the shades and scenes, is not remarkable. Millions sadly suffer the same and worse every.

What is remarkable, is how these very circumstances produced the awakening and extraordinary events that followed. We are all the same, different only in form and function, we all have within us the same divine love and peace. George understands that the purpose of the dark is to make the light shine brighter – and that the light is accessible to all.

Above all else, this biography hopes to bring hope.

When you have eliminated the impossible

"Don't tell me your name! Don't tell me anything about you," George Lawson *firmly ordered down the phone. "Just come and we'll talk."*

I did as commanded and turned up outside George's apartment block in Grays. George happened to be approaching the entrance just as I got to it; he was returning from the supermarket, could easily have been out when I called and I would have driven away. I have long since stopped believing in coincidence.

It was a long string of "coincidences" that led me, the arch rationalist, deeply fascinated by the science of quantum physics, mind and consciousness, to step into a study of Spiritualism. Being recommended to George by my new and good friend Carol Long at The Beacon of Light (thanks, Carol) was just another example of extraordinary synchronicities I had enjoyed in the months since my dear wife retreated from physicality. But this is not my story; my introduction is merely to add to the swollen volumes of testimonials to George's ability.

During our chat about this and that, after some quiet meditation for both of us, George channelled my beloved wife, my mother, my father and even my dear late brother. He "got" my wife's unique name and my initials, communicating personality, facts and descriptions that were unique to my beloved, to each of my family in "spirit." (I prefer to call them Eternal Energies, to strip some of the pre-Einstein patina and "spookiness" around the phenomenon of extra-physical existence.)

George mentioned, for example, an incident on holiday in County Mayo when I drove away from the shops without realising my wife wasn't in the back seat. George knew nothing about me and even close family would *not have known about this incident. His communication included mention of a visit to Knock Cathedral, and how it had deeply impressed my wife, and an argument on the seashore – although arguments with my strong-minded angel were hardly rare.*

Since my extraordinary epiphany to explore Spiritualism, I have been training to meditate and raise sensitivity and intuition; the presence of their energies was almost palpable and their personalities unmistakable. But there was more.

"I've been told to give you the manuscript of my biography," George said, as we were winding up. We agreed that he would email me a PDF of the first draft of early years, before he embarked on his own mediumship and message, kindly transcribed by Pauline Piper; thanks for your patient work, Pauline.

A few days later, after some discussion by phone and emails, George rang me late one evening. He blessed me with an unsolicited telephone reading from my beloved, again with details, language and personality that were unmistakable.

"I want you to write the book," George said, "I've been told to give the whole thing to you. It's yours."

Writing has been a passion poorly pursued by me. I have two unfinished books, one about a minicab driving sleuth and another an adult fairy tale love story. I had discussed with my wife how I would love to make a living from writing, having retired from teaching.

To find myself writing the biography of one of the more eminent mediums, is beyond chance and coincidence, to me. Not only is it the opportunity to write something that stands a chance of being read – George is globally known for his gift – it combines the two life-streams that currently are converging for me.

The coincidences continued as I began to re-write Pauline's work: incidents and personalities that resonated almost precisely with some of my own experience and life, as if I was meant to write about them.

My childhood was spent absorbing spiritual practice, prayer and legendary tales from my grandfather, whilst my father encouraged relentlessly rational and reasoned science.

Spiritualism itself is about the only place where I can routinely observe the phenomena of extra-dimensional existence. In my view, these are strongly indicated by quantum theories – all atoms are empty space and fundamental particles are multi-dimensional. A pioneer and founder of the Spiritualist "religion" (by legal requirement), Sir Arthur Conan Doyle, had Sherlock Holmes declare: "When you have eliminated the impossible, whatever remains, however improbable, must be the truth." Current science and quantum physics, nascent noetics, confirm that reality is greater than the 4D space time human senses experience.

The demonstrations I have witnessed, the "readings" I have received, convince me beyond doubt. I have eliminated the impossible – there is no fakery or foul play amongst people I know to be genuine and honourable.

Improbable though it may seem, there is eternal life for all. My own mission is to spread the good news.

I hope I have justified the faith placed in me by George and my immortals.

Bob Mallick, 31 October, 2018

Lena and Frank

They could not have been more different.

Lena Wilson, eldest of three children born to George and Christine Wilson, grew up in a tenement flat on Heron Street, Glasgow. Her parents both worked long hours as tanners in the local leatherworks.

It was a Protestant area, in a city where sectarian identity was woven deep into life and culture. The fierce rivalry between Catholic Celtic supporters and Protestant Rangers supporters is only one example of a tension that runs through generations.

Wild war child

Her early years clouded by news of war, with many in the estate losing fathers, uncles, even brothers, added recklessness about life to her maverick nature. The company of the lads in the neighbourhood suited Lena's independent spirit and sense of adventure as she grew up. She was no "girly-girl."

This liking for male company grew as she got older and her fondness for fun and adventure inevitably turned into a fondness for drink. Alcohol was the fun drug of the day and the estate where she played was awash with it. Scotland's affection for alcohol – "whisky" itself derives from the Gaelic for "Water of Life" – runs as deep into the culture even as sectarianism. Catholic and Protestant alike share a fondness for a wee dram!

Alcohol and men would be Lena's orbit and ordeal for the rest of her turbulent life.

Blonde, beautiful and bright, Lena did well at school and went to work as a Personal Assistant in the City. She loved socialising, which meant drinking, flirting easily with the boys she met – most "decent" girls didn't go to pubs back in the day.

Her parents' dismay was no deterrent, nor the disapproval of her sister Margaret, which lasted right to the end of their days. Her greatest affection at home was lavished on George, her brother, the baby of the family.

Officer and gentleman

Francis Lawson, Frank, was born to a well-heeled Catholic family, privately educated and went on to serve in the Royal Navy, a Chief Petty Officer by the age of twenty-two. So far, so satisfying to his middle-class parents, especially his mother, small in stature but formidable in her domination of the family; a good name in the neighbourhood the very highest priority.

Until the mad magic moment he met Lena, Frank's horizons were bounded by his parents' wishes – his mother's commands – and the cosy middle class values of the families around. Lena was a universe apart from the nice neighbourhood girls being raised to be nice mothers, with dolls and sewing and cooking as their main entertainment.

Opposites attract

A Protestant girl from the tenements and a Catholic man from the well-heeled end of town. A flirtatious, wild young girl and a serious young man who looked like Frank Sinatra. They could not have been more different.

The attraction of opposites was instant and irresistible when they met in 1954, Lena out drinking with friends, Frank on shore leave in his smart white officer uniform.

The passion was powerful, too, physically irresistible. Lena became pregnant. Six months later they were married; neither Catholic nor Protestant would countenance the shame of unwed motherhood. And Frank did not want his first child to be called a bastard, as he surely would, in the Glasgow of the 1950s.

Neither family was comfortable with the match, especially Frank's mother. She chose to be estranged from her son and Frank's parents did not make much effort to engage with their grandchildren.

The couple moved into a tenement flat in a block just up from Lena's parents, where Francis was born in January, 1955. When George was born in May, the following year, Lena was twenty one and Frank just twenty-four.

The move from balmy middle class neighbourhood to the humble Protestant streets troubled Frank, his mother's rants ringing in his mind, but not enough to dim his devotion to his amazing, wild, young love. And he would be at sea most of the time; having Lena's family minutes away would be great support and help for the young mum.

The support turned out to be near enough full time.

Being full-time mother to two toddlers was not easy for the vivacious spirit of Lena. Her social whirl was only slightly slowed by motherhood. Her parents took on ever more of the childcare chores. Relations between Lena, her parents and her sister Margaret, chalk to Lena's cheese, grew ever more tense and fractious. The sibling tension lasted to the end.

Civvy street

Frank left the navy and a very short time later, Lena and Frank welcomed their third son, Kenneth, in 1959.

Civilian life was a struggle for Frank, without the regime and order of naval service. Finding well-paid work in Glasgow was nigh impossible and money was tight; too tight to fund the fun and frolics that delighted Lena. And Frank, after years in the navy, was no stranger to alcohol himself.

Three children in one tiny flat, with two parents squandering money on booze, erratic childcare, eventually came to the attention of the social services.

In 1960, Lena and Frank's three children were taken into foster-care. At a time when child safeguarding was not as rigorous as it is today, things had to be pretty bad for such drastic intervention.

Frank persuaded Lena to leave Scotland with him and go to England to find regular work and get their children back.

Frank finally found his feet: a job in the site office at Costain, building the West Thurrock power station. It came with accommodation, a small caravan on the site. A long way from the leafy lanes of his childhood, but a home and a job and a community of others who lived the same modest lives on the site.

Reunited, again

Three months after they were taken away, the three children were collected by their parents. The small, cramped caravan, cold and rattling in bad weather, was a far cry from even the tenement in Glasgow. But they were happy to be back together as a family – and there was a decent pub a short walk away for Lena and Frank.

The caravan was their home for a year and the Lawsons enjoyed the sense of belonging and community with their neighbours. Arthur, a widower and a local at the pub with whom the couple spent a lot of time, offered the family accommodation in his own home.

It was even closer to the pub and, predictably, there was rarely ever enough money to provide any but the bare essentials, after the booze and binges. To fund their habit, Frank had been dipping into the tea money at the site office. Suspicions were beginning to be aroused. Rather than risk being found out, Frank resigned his job at Costain and got a job at the main Post Office, in Grays, the local town. It was a steady job, with good pay and conditions, security for life – a life that looked set to get better and brighter.

For a drinker, they say, one drink is too many and a million isn't enough. Most of the new income went the same way as the old. All too often, Arthur had to subsidise essentials and was often left, literally, holding the babies.

Frank and Lena started running up debts. And still there wasn't enough money for the fun and frolics.

Lena was not to be denied. She allowed herself to be picked up by men in bars, for the drinks they would buy her and the presents they would bring.

Frank, who could not imagine a life without Lena, grew bitter and jealous and drank yet more heavily. He became violent, assaulting Lena and also venting his fury on their two older boys.

Break up, make up...

Whenever life with Frank became unbearable, Lena escaped to her parents in Scotland, not always with her children. She wasn't looking for the solace or comfort of her family, just the chance to take up with her old circle of drinkers and merrymakers.

If she did take her boys with her, they would be dumped with her parents while she disappeared for days on end. If she could, she would spend time with her old flame. But she was not bothered, so long as the man she was with had the price of a drink.

Deliberately or simply in a state of blackout, a kind of waking unconsciousness amongst women with a high tolerance of alcohol that is only now being understood, Lena was oblivious to her family's exasperation.

She seemed utterly without concern for her children, wherever they happened to be. Once, she even brought one of the men back to her family home – and was promptly ejected by her horrified mother.

Done with fun, she would head back to Essex, the boys just more baggage to drag around, with barely more sense of care. The boys were a burden to be borne, a duty to be done – or diverted to the nearest handy help.

A doting Frank, full of remorse, would welcome her with tears and fears, showering her with gifts and good times, no expense spared. Fun, frolic, fight, flight, forgive – for four years the recklessness rollercoasted on.

Until Frank was arrested.

To fund the frenzy in the old familiar way, he had been embezzling from the Post Office. He was convicted and sent to Ford Open Prison, where he would serve two years. Lena visited, sometimes with the boys, but only when she could spare the time and the cash for the fare.

When the visits eventually stopped altogether, Frank attempted suicide by slashing his wrists. It made not a jot difference to his wild and wanton wife.

Without Frank, Lena's liking of men and booze became a growing need. She stayed out longer and more often, with Arthur beginning to lose patience. He asked her to leave; Lena and the boys were rehomed by the council.

Lena tried her best to make a fresh start, got a job at the local café; but the habit had her in its grip. Soon, most of her meagre money was again spent on alcohol. Now Lena drank at home, often with a man, bottles of sherry piling up. No prison visits for Frank, the fare needed for more drink. The boys were left to fend for themselves; stealing what they could from the local shops and market stalls, staying out as long as they could, dreading what might be waiting for them at home.

... *and break up again*

When Frank came home, two years on, the Lawsons were a family again. Frank found full time work. but things were different. Lena and Frank were strained, distant with each other. Whatever spark had kept their manic marriage together, seemed stilled,

Barely weeks after his homecoming, Lena left Frank.

She left him for Dave, a regular at the pub – and one of the regulars in her company at the bar and at her home. Dave worked hard and, like many in physical work, drank hard and big. He was physical in his fury as well, when he lashed out, drunk beyond control, at his new live-in lover. If there is any truth in the view that victims of abuse keep attracting the same personality over and over again, Lena would prove it. Her dissipation had a way yet to go.

Frank was utterly destroyed, losing the woman who had dominated his life since the mad moment in Glasgow, filled his thoughts every single sorry second of his two years in prison. All his futures vanished in an instant, fear and jealousy and loss hitting where it would hurt most.

Work and the children kept him occupied but drink became his comfort and need, the company of his pub mates gave him the moral support. Anger, despair, and loss grew as did his consumption of alcohol. The boys lived in fear of the beating and tirades that usually followed. That Lena lived close by and knew many of the same people in the same drinking holes did not make things easier to bear.

When he could bear it no longer, Frank decided to take his son Kenneth and return home to Scotland. His father had died during Frank's prison sentence and his brother, Barry was posted abroad in the army. Mum was more than happy to have her boy back, with Kenneth as a bonus. Frank was content in the middle class neighbourhood, too, and remained in leafy Dunoon with his mother to the end of her days.

...and again.

Dave, meanwhile, had abandoned Lena, lured by a life in Australia, but she stayed on in his house. Kenneth came back to live with her, but she saw nothing of her two older boys, living in lodgings close by. She was oblivious to to this absence and even the death of her father was but a blip on her permanent pursuit of men and booze.

Men came and men went, a stream of "uncles" for young Kenneth, until Dave's family found a way to force her out of his house. No problem for Lena. She was seeing Bill, a well-off, much older man who lived just across the way and moved in with him – and his Staffordshire Bull Terrier, Ben. For a few years, Lena and Jim and Kenneth lived a steady life, with a steady stream of drink and the pub a daily duty.

After one bout of long and heavy drinking, the dog attacked Lena and bit off her nose. She was taken to hospital for reconstructive surgery and refused to return to Bill's home and the ferocious Ben. Kenneth was carted around various friends until she was again rehoused by the council, in a small flat in Tilbury. The older boys were no longer any part of her life.

Different stage for the same old script: Lena's life returned to the roundabout of drinking and casual pickups, until she met Pat. A heavy drinker himself, Pat was never violent towards Lena and she seemed contented and settled. All day drinking in the safety of the flat was common, often with a gang of friends to keep things rolling.

But drink is one of the commonest causes of aggression and violence, as any court or casualty ward will testify. A woman at one of the all-day sessions snapped suddenly, rushed into the kitchen for a carving knife and stabbed Pat as he sat smug on the sofa, killing him instantly.

Ravaged by booze and a shiftless, turbulent life, Lena at fifty now looked like a scrawny seventy. She lived in Pat's flat with Kenneth until January 1989. Now fifty-three, Lena spent some time in hospital and eventually came home. A few days later, Kenneth returned from night shift to find her dead in bed.

She was cremated at Upminster Crematorium, with financial help from her family in Scotland.

Two years later, on Christmas Day 1991, Frank Lawson died alone at his home in Dunoon. He was sitting in the chair studying the television guide, when he succumbed to fluid in his lungs. He was buried in Dunoon, on the 9th January 1992 – his son Francis's birthday.

Both Lena and Frank had stopped drinking for a while before they died, both died alone, and both died with nothing to leave behind, no photographs or mementos to mark their lives and times.

The child

Heron Street

George loved his mother. Not unusual, because our mother's face is the first we fall in love with, having grown to life under her very heart. In George's case, circumstances made the bond even stronger.

His father was away in the navy most of the time. His brother, Francis, was living with Lena's mother, so there was just the two of them. Petite and brilliantly blonde, Lena's beautiful face lit up George's heart when she smiled. All of his attention and devotion was directed at Lena. She was his world and no one else counted.

George loved visiting his grandparents, too, though not too fond of Auntie Margaret, who was always arguing with his mum. He was especially fond of his uncle, Lena's beloved younger brother, George. It tickled him that his uncle had the same name. Lena was not as amused, because he was the third George in the immediate living family. She chose to use his second name, Frederick, which she made sure was shortened to Rick, not plain old Fred. Lena did nothing by the book. To his family and old friends, George is still Ricky.

Life in the tenement flat was modest in the extreme. None of the Heron Street flats had a bath, the public baths in Ruby Street the place for that special treat. Most tenants used tin baths filled with hot water from kettles and pans. Lena bathed George in the kitchen sink as he watched the children play in the schoolyard opposite the window.

There was no toilet in the flat either. Each block had just one shared toilet, on the ground floor; scraps of newspaper on a nail served as toilet tissue. For George, creeping in the dark to the cold loo downstairs was always an experience to dread. In the flickering shadows and whistling wind, he fancied he saw people and heard voices that were scary for a little boy.

But George had his mum and he was happy.

Things began to change when his father left the navy for the irregular and uncertain civilian world. Frank was restless without the order and discipline of the senior service and life at home was often tense. But Francis was back with the family and, soon, his brother Kenneth was born. George enjoyed the bustle and the feeling of being a family, despite his parents' descent into drink and dissolution and daily dramas.

Suddenly, everything changed.

Separation

Social services became aware of the drunk and dysfunctional Lawson family. Francis, George and baby Kenneth were taken away from their parents and handed to a foster mother, Peggy, for their care and well-being.

The terror was overwhelming, the loss and isolation unbearable for a child unable to express his feelings in words.

Three-year old George was distraught almost constantly. Oxfordshire seemed utterly alien from Glasgow, a world away in both distance and lifestyle.

George pined for his mother, his grandparents and uncle, the familiar sights, sounds and smells of the only home he knew. The seeds of resentment germinated in this feeling of being abandoned and rejected. Having his brothers with him was some comfort, but he felt desperately alone in bed every night of his time with the foster family.

The turmoil at home was routine, he couldn't understand why his parents couldn't be with them. Not knowing if he would ever see them again was a deep and fearful pain. Mum had been his world, why did she not come for him?

Peggy was a large lady, with two children of her own. They were a good family and she was kind to George and his brothers. With five youngsters to manage, Kenneth just a baby with a deformity in his feet into the bargain, Peggy had to run the home with strict rules and routine. George didn't like being controlled, used to doing pretty much as he pleased back in Bridgetown. His lifelong resistance to authority probably began in that cosy confinement in Oxfordshire.

The Lawson brothers were with Peggy for three months. For a three-year old, it felt like a long, lonely lifetime.

Frank and Lena came to get their children, taking them for a walk in the park to tell them about their new life: the family would remain in England, in West Thurrock. Father was helping to build a big new power station.

Home is where the heart is

A caravan on a building site, huddled amongst a village of caravans; their new home was even humbler and sparser than the tenement in Heron Street. But it was home and the family was together and George needed nothing more. And Frank had a steady job as Clerk-of-Works in the site office, with a big company. Costains was building a new coal-fired power station and the boys spent hours watching the big machines and armies of men go about their work.

It was boom time for the eighteen miles of Thames riverfront that comprised Thurrock, teeming with factories and warehouses, two oil refineries, three cement factories and the Port of Tilbury, throbbing with the constant flow of ships and tankers. Thurrock today is totally transformed, two-thirds residential developments encircling the massive magnet of Lakeside Retail Park – once a chalk quarry.

In their small, cream-and-green caravan, Calor Gas for cooking, heating and gas-mantle lighting, George wallowed in the closeness of the family together. The site really was like a small village, with other families on similar meagre means. A patch of derelict land was an adventure playground and stadium for the children, where George first tasted the delight of kicking a football.

Francis started school at the local primary, George and Kenneth got places at a nursery. Freed from childcare chores and less crowded in the day, Lena also seemed happy with the new life and sense of community.

George first became aware of death with two fatal accidents, one on the nearby railway line and another when a workman fell off the towering pylon the boys were watching erected.

George was much more upset by the discovery of a bag of drowned kittens on the site. They had been drowned by one of his playmates. George's distress was magnified by the fear that he may be blamed for it, until his friend owned up to the offence.

Arthur

After about a year on the site, in 1961, the Lawsons moved in with Arthur, a widower who had become friends with Frank and Lena – and the boys hanging outside the pub where they all drank. Arthur's three-bed-room house was like a mansion after the cramped caravan and George loved it.

He started school and enjoyed that, too, bright and eager to learn, doing well like both his parents before him. Those early years, between four and seven, were stable and the parents' "socialising" didn't affect the boys too much.

Lena's parents were able to come down for visits; Nan short and plump, indulging her grandchildren, and gaunt grandad, who spent much of his time in bed with breathing problems. They always brought presents and took the boys out to the shops, for days out at the seaside, to the park for picnics and play.

Bus trips to the cinema in Grays were another treat, right from the start, when Frank asked for one and three half tickets. George would watch fascinated as the conductor took the money, keyed in the numbers in his waist-mounted machine, cranked the handle to spit out their ticket strip, pressing a lever to neatly trim it from the roll.

There were no less than three theatres in the town: the Regal, the Ritz and the State. Ice cream from the usherette's tray was a highlight of any film, George preferring tubs of ice cream with spoons, dad always went for orange ice lollies, Lena and the other boys choosing ice creams with wafers.

Grays bustled with shops and market stalls, the Queens Hotel as the centrepiece, its bars and ballroom open to the public. George and his brothers lapped it all up. But family trips gradually grew less frequent, as their parents spent more of their time drinking and socialising, money growing ever tighter. When they did get to see a film, the boys invariably went to a matinee on their own.

Uncle George

Uncle George, his mum's younger brother, came down from Scotland with his friends Bernard and Ricky. They were looking for work and stayed with Arthur and the Lawsons – a tight squeeze, but the laughter and fun made this time a delight for George. Frank found them work on his site and eventually they found their own rented accommodation.

Frank and Lena had begun to become unsettled with each other, their drinking taking up more and more of their time and money, their heated arguments frequent and frightening for the boys. For the two years that George and his brothers stayed at Arthur's, they kept things calm.

That Christmas was a complete joy, for George and his brothers. His uncle and his friends showered them with presents, including a bicycle, for which they had to hunt all over the house and garden, following clues given out during the day.

George and Bernard eventually returned to Scotland, but Ricky stayed behind. He had met Dawn and went on to marry her, raise a family and provide an ever-welcoming refuge in Thurrock for George. Ricky was always reaching out to help and advise George, and he became very close to their family, a bond that remains strong even after Ricky's passing in 2008.

Anger cocktail

The hostility and tensions hidden while Uncle George stayed with them, surfaced with a vengeance. Lena's liking of male company and attention, flirting and often going out with men friends without Frank, began eating away at her husband. Alcohol and jealousy made a dangerous cocktail.

The children saw Frank get increasingly violent towards Lena. George understood nothing of this, only the deep sadness, fear and distress of seeing his father beat the mother he adored

George woke in alarm.

"No!" Francis was screaming hoarsely. "Stop it! STOP IT!"

"GET BACK TO BED!" His father's yell shaking through the flat with the slur of heavy drinking..

Francis ran back to bed, trembling and whimpering. All had gone utterly quiet downstairs. Francis couldn't stay put. He grabbed George and led him, running, down the stairs, flinging open the door to the front room.

The scene before him would etch itself deep into George's heart and mind.

His mother was sprawled on the sofa, twisting and kicking frantically as Frank twisted a yellow scarf tight around her slender throat. Lena was making choking, guttural sounds, face turning white and purple with veins, eyeballs near to popping from their sockets.

Francis charged at his father with all the force he could muster. It seemed to shake Frank aware. He loosened his grip on the scarf and Lena dropped to the floor, gasping, heaving – but alive.

Bedtime, bad time

Fear caused George to begin wetting the bed at night. Wanting to pee is a natural reflex to fear, but George also feared venturing out of the bed for what he may find outside. A drunken Frank could lay into you for any reason or none at all.

George tried to conceal the problem at first. He switched places with his brothers so they might be blamed; he tried to hide the soiled sheets; turned the mattress over, but discovery was inevitable. As was Frank's fury and frustration – which, of course, made the fear and peeing problem worse.

George still wouldn't leave his bed and his brothers' complaint usually brought Lena. She would soothe him, stroke his forehead. and change the sheets without a fuss. Frank would usually lie in bed, ignoring the uproar, but occasionally he would roar through the door, shove Lena aside and drag George out of bed for a pitiless beating.

They took him to the doctor, who handed them a machine that would buzz when George's bladder was full. It didn't work; the problem was deeper than a full bladder, the fear and distress and dark dreams of a little boy.

Whatever the season, the boys were sent up to bed promptly at six, under strict orders not to leave the room for any reason. Lena and Frank would then head off to the pub; not for them the bother and cost of a babysitter. If they gave any thought to the danger of fire or other emergency, the pub and partying were prime priority for the parents. The long, bright summer evenings were the worst for the boys: hard to sleep with the light through the the thin curtains and the sights and sounds of other children happily playing outside.

Often, Lena and Frank would bring a crowd back from the pub with them, clanking bags of bottles to supply all-night drinking sessions.

For the boys, sleep was fitful. Loud voices, drunken singing, doors banging – and more agony for George, who couldn't go to the toilet even if he wanted to, without fear of discovery.

He feared for his mother every single night after watching her almost strangled to death – who could predict how and when Frank's jealous rage would vent next?

Losing Lena

Lena would escape to Scotland and her parents' home when the violence and oppressive jealousy got too much for her. She didn't always take the boys with her, leaving them to the volatile violence of their fearsome father. Each time, George became deeply anxious, fearful that he would never see his beloved Mum again – those were the words she screamed at Frank, after all.

Losing Lena would be unbearable; George still remembered the pain of separation during his time in foster care. He clung to her ever closer, buying her presents with his pitiful pocket money even though she chided him for it.

On one of her escapes, Lena took George with her instead, leaving Francis and Kenneth with Frank. George barely saw his mother after the first day or so; she was off carousing for days, with an old lover she saw every time she returned to Glasgow. George was awakened one night by Nan Wilson screaming.

"Get that man out of here!" She shouted. "And I want you out of the house in the morning." Lena had brought her lover home, expecting him to stay there with her.

Lena rushed into George's bedroom, got him dressed, grabbed their luggage and stormed out of the house. "We're going to Dunoon," she told George.

It was George's first experience of how her mother used her wiles to win favours with men. They had missed the ferry, so she flirted with an American sailor, persuading him to take them on the naval launch that was taking him across to his Dunoon base. George watched as his mother kissed and cuddled with the utter stranger, who marched off to his base once they reached the far shore.

Lena was not the only victim of Frank's fists. The boys were beaten, too, and frequently. The slightest fault or failing, or even none at all, would bring the boot or buckle or bare, hard knuckle. Nine-year old George bore the brunt of the beatings, because he would rush to protect Lena; it may also have been because George was the spitting image of his mum.

Francis spent most of his time hiding under the stairs and keeping out of the way, not helping at all, and Kenneth was just six, so perhaps George was the only one handy for a hit. Lena could not intervene. For George the feeling of being rejected and abandoned was overwhelming.

Birthday to beat

George was delighted with the set of dynamo-powered bike lights his parents got him for his birthday. They were powered by little gizmos clipped to turn with the wheels, needing no batteries. Kenneth, too small for the bike, sneaked it out of the garden for a ride and, inevitably, fell off it. The bike lights were smashed. Not telling George about it and hoping not be discovered, Kenneth sneaked the bike back into the garden.

Frank saw the bike when he came home from work. His fury rose fast when he saw the broken lights. He charged up the stairs, roaring with rage, dragging George out from the bath, dragging him down the stairs, slapping his wet skin so it stung and hitting him about the head. He flung George, naked and wet, out into the biting winter cold of the garden. He was left there until Lena brought him in, wrapped him in a towel and led him upstairs past Frank's glowering menace in the living room.

Kenneth confessed to George later that night, when the boys were in bed. He offered to confess to the accident and take his own punishment, but George could see no point in both being beaten for the one broken birthday bike.

The Lawson boys suffered their ordeal separately, each locked inside his own way of dealing with the horror. The family didn't ever gather to laugh and chat and share news and experiences, each a unit separate from all others. This sense of separation would survive in the siblings long after their parents passed.

Each unit of the Lawson household was functioning in an almost robotic, automatic way, one day indistinguishable from the next. Even the rows and volatility were routine, respecting no special events or celebrations. Weekends were no different, no cause for cheer.

School solace and sweets

School was escape. That would have been enough reason for George to enjoy his time there, but he genuinely did enjoy learning. He basked in the praise when he worked hard and did well, because home never offered any praise or support.

Hardly an angel – Mr Stewart the headmaster had to dish out corporal punishment to George frequently enough – George's efforts even earned him a book prize one year. His parents seemed completely unmoved and oblivious. They kept no mementos or photographs at all. Even their wedding photographs, which they allowed to be defaced by the kids' crayons, did not survive them. George and his brothers would never be able to share any happy snaps – or even glum ones – with anyone, ever.

The Lawson lads found any way they could to stay away from the house where their very presence seemed to irritate and infuriate their parents. They loitered the streets, kicked a ball around the recreation ground, played Cowboys and Indians with home-made bows and arrows. Their friends would return to comforting, supportive families and homes, George and his brothers to bedroom curfew and an atmosphere electric with menace and fear.

November gave them a chance to stay up and out later, to collect a "Penny for the Guy" outside the pub where their parents propped the bar. Drunks can be generous – or careless – with loose change and the boys did well. Carol singing at Christmas was also a welcome extension of their absence from internment – and a handy earner. Most of the money was spent in Skinner's sweet shop, a cornucopia of confectionery-crammed jars.

George chose light, milk-flavoured gums that come in the shape of tiny milk bottles, which he considered better value than heavy boiled sweets He developed a lifelong passion for chocolate in all its delightful variations and creations.

Skinners was the scene of another sad and deeply shocking moment for George and his brothers.

Jock was the adorable little Golden Retriever puppy the Lawson lads had received as a rare gift in their barren days. They had taken Jock with them on the trip to town for sweets. Skinners allowed Jock in because the boys carried him, as did so many lady customers with toy breeds. On the way out, the boys put Jock down to dig into the sweet bag. Little Jock ran across the road and was hit by a car. He got up, limped painfully back to the Lawson's front gate, where he collapsed and passed away.

Cubs, camps – and football

For George and Francis, joining the Cubs was a liberation and utterly engaging. Like most things once his interest was aroused, George threw himself into the meetings, the badges and knots and team tasks, with gusto. He became a pack leader in short order. The added bonus was the camping trips, whole days away from home with other boys. The Condovers campsite on Tilbury Marsh wasn't far away, but far enough to feel like sweet freedom.

Being away from the house was always welcome relief, in whatever form it came, and Cubs was about as good as it got.

Apart from football.

Football would weave in and out of George's life, and it was his comfort and pleasure at West Thurrock Primary School.

George and Francis loved to play the beautiful game whenever and wherever they could. George's head was often pounding with the dull pain of heading the heavy leather ball, one with an inner tube and protruding laces. They played at every break in school. When Francis moved up to Aveley Secondary School, George would wait outside the gates for him for the essential daily dose of their favourite escape.

Their usual haunt was a the recreation ground nearby. It was a public space, open to every man and his dog – or just a dog on its own. A stray Alsatian took a shine to George, as dogs and other animals still do. The huge beast was as gentle as a puppy with George, holding his hand in its mouth as they ran around the field. If George wandered too far, the dog chased after him to herd him back.

One of his playmates told George that the dog was part of a pair belonging to a local farmer, but George decided to take him home. The farmer could just think the dog had run away, or been run over, he reasoned; his fault for letting it run loose. A year on from the shock of Jock struck outside Skinners, this friendly giant would surely help to heal the hurt.

Such pragmatic reasoning, self-serving and oblivious of obligation or outcome, or the impact on others, was typical for a child growing up by living off his wits, used to looking out for himself. There was precious little parental mentoring on morality in the limited communication at home.

His parents did realise the impact of keeping such a conspicuous canine in a small town – George's mate wouldn't be the only person to know whose dog it was. They didn't want any trouble with local farmers, who might have mates where the Lawsons drank. They persuaded George to take the dog back to a grateful and astonished farmer, surprised such a small boy could handle his ferocious Alsatian.

The affection and joy he felt with Jock the puppy, the gentle giant Alsatian and the new Jock his parents eventually bought, awoke a love for animals. The love for all animals amplified as George continued his adventures and misadventures with humans.

Holiday of a lifetime

The Lawsons went on holiday as a family just once.

Frank had secured a steady job at the main Post Office in Grays. It was a coveted job, steady employment with the government, more money – spare cash, until the carousing caught up. The Lawsons remained lodging with Arthur, helping ease the family finances further.

Nan Wilson, visiting from Scotland, joined the Lawsons on this singular excursion, to bracing air of the Norfolk Broads. Frank, flaunting his naval experience, sported a captain's cap as he commandeered the cruiser they had rented for the week, the *Prelude 5*.

It was, of course, a drinking holiday for the adults, with pub stops at every opportunity and a huge supply of booze on the boat. George and the boys loved the adventure and rarely spent a day without getting soaked themselves – by the water, not the booze! For all the fun, George dreaded being out on open water with his drunken dad at the helm.

Doubts about his father's understanding of the ways of water seemed confirmed when the family tied up at a quay to visit a quaint rural pub. When they returned to the boat, they found it aground, hanging askew from the rope that had tied it to the quay. Frank Lawson, master of the seas, had failed to take account of the tides on the waterway they were using. They had no option but to wait for the tide to return and refloat their boat.

Captain Lawson also presided over an engine fire on the boat, which needed another boat to come to their rescue. Nan Wilson remembered to grab her bottle of whisky, never mind her life jacket was on lopsided and back to front!

The comic captaincy was capped on the final day when Frank Lawson was stung on the neck by a wasp, yelping and raging with pain. Francis and George scurried to hide – they did *not* want Frank to see them laughing at their father's fury. Schadenfreude triumphed over any shred of sympathy in the sons of Captain Lawson.

Indecent assault

The early years of Frank's work at the Post Office were relatively contented and the children saw more presents than they ever had before, at birthdays and Christmas and other feast days. George got a brand new pair of football boots. He was sure they made him play better, just like the ads promised. The ad hoc gifts of affluence apart, life continued with the same lack of affection and communication as before. The Lawson parents steadily increased the frequency and volume of their drinking.

The family also made regular trips to Southend-on-Sea, but not for the fun of sand castles and sea splashing. The parents made straight for their favourite piano bar, where they would spend the whole day drinking and singing with other regulars. There were no other children in the group, so the brothers were left to their own devices, with a handful of money to find their own fun. This they did happily enough, enjoying arcade games, candy floss and rides on the seafront funfair.

Frank and Lena seemed oblivious to any possibility of misadventure falling on three young boys wandering a town of transients completely unsupervised. The brothers kept together, for company and safety, until the night George needed to pee.

The toilets were tucked away in a dark corner of the seafront. George did not notice the man who followed him into the lavatory; he had probably been waiting in a dark corner just for a likely victim. George was indecently assaulted, a shocking and fearful experience he would completely block from his mind for years to come. He breathed not a word of it to his brothers or his parents.

Ibrox

The family could also now afford trips to Scotland together, catching up with family and friends – and football in the street for the boys. The local lads mocked their Sassenach accents, but the boys let their football do the talking and soon won them over.

The sectarian rivalry of professional Scottish football was not so easy to overcome.

The Wilsons – grandad and Uncle George – were devout supporters of the Protestant Rangers, regular pilgrims to their hallowed home, Ibrox. Frank Lawson, a Catholic, was joined by Uncle Richie (Lena's sister Margaret had also married outside the Protestant persuasion) in the ritual passion for Celtic, at Park Head.

George absorbed the Rangers religion, growing up in the Wilson home. But his most memorable live game was a treat from Uncle Richie, who took George and Kenneth to a Celtic home game at Park Head. The two boys switched faith to Celtic from that day; Francis continued to visit Ibrox and follow Rangers with Uncle George.

All three brothers were at Ibrox Park for the old-firm derby on 2 January, 1971, when railings collapsed on Stairwell 13 at the end where Rangers supporters were packed. Sixty Rangers supporters lost their lives in the crush and hundreds were injured, some with what now would be called "life-changing" damage.

George, Kenneth and Uncle Richie watched it all unfold from the Celtic end, wondering if Francis and Uncle George were safe at the other. Not until much later, struggling through the pandemonium, they found Francis and Uncle George safe outside the melée. Stairwell 13 was the one they would have used to reach their usual space amongst the Rangers ranks, but Uncle George had been delayed. They had to use a different stairwell.

The mental impact of the event would haunt Scottish football for years, just as much as it affected young George and his brothers; the idea of counselling was not yet common and the horror would remain fresh every time the memory triggered.

The Bully

Playing with their cousins, the children of Aunt Margaret were favourite playmates. George "clicked" with Jim, who was the same age, and Chris, who was the same age as Kenneth. The two squabbling sisters happened not only to marry Catholics but also both give birth to boys in the same year! Margaret's younger two children were too young to join the crew – especially into The Bully.

A disused railway siding over which their tenement estate loomed, The Bully led to a labyrinth of dark tunnels snaking under the streets and buildings, discarded tools and nooks and crannies offering hours of adventure.

When they weren't exploring or hiding and seeking, the boys did what they loved best: play football. There was a green nearby, with proper pitches, but they were made of asphalt, didn't feel right under foot. The brothers and their buddies preferred to play in the street, chalk-scratched lines on building walls for goal posts. The surface felt more natural to George; it also saved time, because the ball bounced back from the wall, goal or miss, and you didn't have to chase it all around the park.

Frank and Lena were rarely with their boys and happy enough that the brothers were away entertaining themselves; the parents' time was spent in a constant and uninterrupted round of drinking with other grownups. They, too, had no shortage of willing playmates.

Sensing spirit

Uncle George and his wife Annette were leaving their lodgings in the Wilson family home to a flat of their own.

On moving day, eleven-year old George went to the new flat with Uncle George, Auntie Annette, Cousin Jim and big brother Francis. Old furniture belonging to the previous tenant had to be cleared. They had a full van load to take to the dump and it was cold and darkening in the late winter afternoon, so George stayed behind to mind the now-empty flat.

The flat was dark, too, because none of the Victorian tenements had electricity. A couple of candles lit the lounge, where some of the nicer old furniture had been retained. George selected a book from the handsome hardwood bookcase and settled down on the floor to read.

George heard the front door open – he had left it unlocked – and sensed that someone had entered the flat. "I'm in here!" George called from the lounge. Hearing no answer, he walked through the hall and closed the front door.

Back in the lounge, he returned to his reading. In a few minutes, he sensed the presence again: a cold energy that came to rest just over his shoulder. The chill was like a whispered breath on his cheek, soundless. The hair on the nape of his neck tingled erect and one of the candles blew out.

George quickly cupped his hands around the other candle. If it blew out, he had no matches to light it again. As he did so, he saw the figure of an old man slinking away. The apparition was dishevelled but not like a street drunk or derelict, more like the hermits or misers George had seen in book illustrations. George sensed that the figure seemed anxious, upset, even angry and wondered if the spectre might be registering upset at the removal of his precious possessions.

George, too, became anxious and was delighted when the others returned from the dump. George told them about the vision and the negative feelings that seemed to come from it. Uncle George was unimpressed. "Ye're away with the the fairies, laddie!" He laughed. But Auntie Annette wasn't so sure; she insisted they leave immediately, without disturbing anything else in the flat. Uncle George knew better than to oppose his strong-willed wife!

Furious Frank

George feared his father as much as he adored his mother. Frank's fury was constantly simmering under the surface and would explode at anyone, anytime, for any reason or no reason at all. Even old Arthur was not immune. Frank was jealous at any sign of affection between his wife and the friend who had opened his house to the Lawsons – precisely because of the affection he felt for them!

Lena didn't help ease the jealousy. Whilst Frank was out at work, she would be off drinking with other men. She might even flaunt some of the gifts they gave her, trinkets and tat. Once she went out with Arthur, who bought her something she claimed to need but couldn't afford. Frank exploded with rage and attacked Arthur , an old man no match for him, with fist and foot.. Arthur took to keeping his own counsel whenever Frank was around – as did the brothers.

Special occasions weren't exempt, either. On his birthday one year, George agreed with Lena that he would bring some friends home after school. They hadn't bargained on Frank being home from work, having a lie-down upstairs. The noise of the boys playing and shouting downstairs roused Frank, who rushed roaring down the stairs, burst into the front room and soundly slapped George around his face, pushing him to floor before he stomped back up. Public humiliation ended any thought of a party.

Losing Lena, again

Drink took its toll on Lena, too, ravaging her face and body, however hard she tried to hide the dissolution. George, who had once adored his beautiful mother, began to feel distant and demoralised, no longer the feeling of closeness and comfort.

He had by now seen her licentious antics on drink more than a few times. The episode in Scotland could not be erased from his mind: his mother being expelled by Nan Wilson for bringing her lover back to the family flat; shamelessly snogging a sailor to steal a ride across the Clyde; shacking up with a taxi driver when Nan Lawson refused to let her stay in Dunoon.

He was old enough now to know that his Mum's behaviour was not right – and to realise that his adoration was no longer returned in kind. His mother was in a world of her own, filled with drink and partying and men, men, men.

The disillusionment affected every part of George's life, because his Mum had been at the very core of it for so long.

School, once a solace and a source of success, suffered badly. It didn't help that Lena, oblivious to George's complaints, insisted that he wear short trousers to school. Long trousers were for secondary school, in her view, and her view could not be shifted. George was mocked, ostracised, picked on, pointed at and even teachers tormented him for tiny faults and errors.

Hurrying back from the toilet one day, buttoning up in haste (no zips back then), George arrived with a tiny wet patch at the front of his shorts. The teacher made him stand on a chair for the whole lesson, as an example of a lazy and careless person, unable to control himself.

Isolated, belittled, constantly churning emotions, alienated from the only love he had known, even the comfort of his brothers could not console little George. At times, the volcano would burst and George would lash out, as he had seen his father do so easily and so often. Like his father, he also hit a girl at school – it was the first but, unlike Frank, the only time for George. The remorse was almost instant and only resolved when, years later, George was blessed to meet the girl, now a young woman, and to apologise for his outrage.

Life without Frank

Suddenly, Frank was no longer around. He had been convicted and sent to prison for embezzling from the Post Office. Serious men in suits had visited several times, but neither parent told them these were plain clothes officers questioning Frank. Lena had even attended court, keeping the whole matter a secret until there was no choice but to tell the boys.

It was George's first encounter with the idea of prison and it wouldn't be his last. For him, relief from the daily fear and torment of his volcanic father was a joyful relief. Concern for Frank barely flickered across his mind. The relief was so immense, the lifting of fear, George stopped wetting the bed at night.

Without Frank's regular income, life became a struggle. Food was scarce and sparse, Lena spending most of her benefit money on drink. At school, George felt intense embarrassment and impatient resentment at lunchtimes, waiting for his free school meal while the other children queued up to pay for theirs. He sunk deeper into his dark isolation.

Moving up to Aveley Secondary School, to join big brother Francis, relieved some of the isolation. George's record at primary school put him in the "A" stream, a status he didn't like because most of his friends were in the "B" stream – bad boys were so much more fun!

Nothing relieved the poverty or the indifference of their mother, her compulsion for the company of men and copious quantities of drink. Lena brought an endless stream of "uncles" home to share her bed.

For a while, Arthur tolerated this behaviour, even dipping into his own small income to help out with food and provisions. When he could take it no longer, he asked Lena to leave.

Aveley

The Lawson brood was settled into a council house in Aveley, close to the elder boys' school. It was a three-bedroomed house. Lena had the biggest bedroom, George and Kenneth had a single bed each in the second and Frank had the third, box room.

It was a luxury for George to have a bed all his own, which remained bone dry every night without any fancy medical machines! The house was never decorated during the time they lived there and furniture was sparse, but it felt a lot better than the cramped conditions at Arthur's home.

George walked to school with Brian, who lived next door and was in the same age and same class. They became good friends and playmates. Brian's dad fixed it for George to come to Maldon Creek for a children's outing run by his working men's club. George prepared for the trip by pilfering petty cash from his mother's purse, to keep up with Brian's pocket money. He also snatched some cigarettes from her bag; Lena would not notice, he knew. He and Brian sloped off to the bushes during the day for sneaky smokes, both not yet in their teens,; it was a time when smoking was advertised as a glamorous, adventurous, grown up pleasure, no health scares back then.

Lena made an effort to improve life, for herself and her children. She got a job as a waitress, at a transport café on the A13 arterial road that skirted Aveley. Work is the curse of the drinking classes, the saying goes:

Lena's long love for alcohol soon subsumed the new life. She took to drinking at home because her old haunts in Grays were too far away. Sherry became her staple, empty bottles of it hidden all over the house–cupboards, kitchen drawers, under piles of linen – vainly hoping to hide her addiction from her boys.

Her fondness for male attention hadn't abated either. A steady stream of "uncles" came and went while Frank was not available. One, a painter and decorator George had to call "Uncle Phil," was around for almost a year, though it made no difference to the mess and dilapidation of the flat. And Phil didn't have exclusive access to Lena, who entertained all comers as the fancy took her.

The boys became an irritant, irrelevant when Mum entertained. George found Francis, one day, kicking at the front door in silent fury. Lena had locked all the entrances to have privacy to party. Francis gave one last, frustrated kick at the door and skulked away without a word to George. The boys had all grown separate from each other, in their own silent torment.

Alienation

George's alienation from his once-adored Mum grew daily. He was ashamed of being with her, embarrassed by her distracted behaviour, heartbroken by her complete lack of care and affection, bewildered by the succession of men lurching in and slipping out of their lives. When Francis wasn't around, George took to vent his frustrated feelings by bullying and sometimes even beating young Kenneth.

The two older boys found ways to feed the family when their mother failed to provide, which was most of the time. George would follow the early morning milkman as he delivered milk, eggs, bread and other staples – and steal them back home to feed his brothers.

The farm nearby was handy for plucking up potatoes and the boys got very good at finding edible mushrooms in the woods. For a whole fortnight, they feasted on just mushrooms, testing George's growing skill as a cook. It wasn't great food, but Lena was rarely in any shape to cook anything at all. School dinners made up the slack in term times, while Lena lapped on liquor at home.

Nan and grandad Wilson would come down from Scotland to help out, when things got too bad and Social Services intervention loomed, when Lena's alcoholism led to stays in hospital. The grandparents showed little care for their daughter, but did all they could for the boys; the household dynamics of Glasgow had just b been transplanted to Essex.

When Nan couldn't make it – she had two jobs to top up her pension and couldn't risk losing them – Uncle George would take time off work to look after them. George, still in his twenties, adored his sister and his nephews, regardless of Lena's illness – he seemed to understand what is now commonplace, that alcoholism is above all a mental illness. He was kind to his sister and little George was more comfortable with that than Nan's coldness. The boys had a much easier time with Uncle George than Nan's strict regime.

Fitting the role

Pilfering whatever he needed was almost a reflex for George. He pinched clothes to make sure he never again stood out as the odd one at school. This craving to fit in, belong, affected his school work. He deliberately

"med" to fit in with the crowd, even failing tests deliberately
…dn't stand out.

George at school and in public was a different personality from
the fuming, frustration of home. He cultivated a swagger, Jack-the-lad
cheek and mischievousness. He sang the hymns at assembly a verse behind everyone else, hid alarm clocks in girls' bags timed to go off as the
prayer was said, defaced posters in Religious Education classes, waggled
fingers in front of the projector at film screenings, taunted teachers with
questions to entertain the troops.

Many teachers refused to have him in class; he would stand outside, sneaking peeks and making faces.

Even getting the cane almost every day just added more bricks for
the wall of bravado George built around his fragile core.

"I'm getting fed up of caning you, Lawson," the exasperated
headmaster said one day.

"Get one of the others to do it, then!" George quipped carelessly
back.

Catholic charity was a saving grace for the boys, books from St
Vincent de Paul often their only present at Christmas. The charity also
took the boys to camp, with a range of activities and pastimes laid on. Fun
or not, George again resented the regimentation, rules and regulation
that bounded his will to do as he pleased. His tough guy persona required
constant feeding of friction with the fathers who ran the camp with Jesuit
order.

Most of the boys at these camps came from troubled or deprived
backgrounds, with pent-up emotions ready to release. Fights were fre-

quent. Boxing matches were arranged to diffuse the distress; when it was his turn in the ring, George contrived to be disqualified from his match by hitting his opponent before the bell.

Grandad appears

Grandad Wilson, who had been ill for many years and barely involved with George and the boys or anyone else, passed away. Lena took the boys up to Bridgetown, to stay with Uncle George, for the funeral.

Family and friends gathered in the front room after the funeral, reminiscing, chatting and, of course, drinking. George sat quietly, watching and listening, tired from a long day. He looked across at the empty chair on which grandad used to sit all day.

It wasn't empty.

Grandad was sitting in his usual chair, looking fitter and smiling warmly at George. Transfixed, frozen by fear, George simply stared, silently. He didn't exclaim or call to any of the others. He didn't want to be branded again as "away with the fairies." He stared at the smiling spirit for long minutes, seeing grandad as clear as if in flesh. Eventually, he looked away and, when his eyes strayed to the chair again, grandad was no longer visible.

George slept with the light on for days after the apparition, before the incident assimilated into indelible memory.

Like so many who eventually awake (and many who don't), fear of ridicule and the weight of life experiences kept this incident dormant in George's mind, like the vision of the unhappy old man in the flat Uncle George had planned to rent.

Children speaking with invisible beings, often loved ones recently passed, is not uncommon; most have it discouraged and learn to live in. the "real" world. Physical apparitions are rare, even amongst long-experienced spiritualists; George had no inkling yet of his natural abilities.

The youth

George was thirteen, well set in his wayward ways amongst his peers, when Frank Lawson returned home from prison. Apart from the rare, brief and boring visits to the prison, George had pretty much put his father out of his mind. Two years is a long time for a boy of eleven.

The probation service got Frank a steady, full-time job on the production line at Thames Board Mills, in Purfleet. He was away most of the time at work, or back in a bar with Lena.

George could sense a change between his parents, more sullen silences, but life at home seemed steady for a while. The experience of prison seemed to have knocked some stuffing out of him.

Football to the fore

Football had been the constant diversion and delight for George, even during the trying times at West Thurrock. For the pleasure to turn into a passion and the pursuit of professionalism, George would forever thank Aveley Secondary Modern – and Mr Harold Napier.

Mr Napier seemed to understand the restless boy. He had seen, from over the lad's shoulder, George mimic his own mannerisms to amuse his mates in a very early class. but he didn't react by excluding him as others did. Mr Napier managed the boys in his sports class with patience and an understanding of how to get *all* the boys engaged, so even the weak and weighty could enjoy a hearty kickabout.

Having been a "pro" himself with West Bromwich Albion, Harold Napier naturally had what today might be called "cred." George could trust the man because he seemed to speak from proper experience. He could relate to the teacher's passion for the game as he got heated and excitable, running about and jumping, white cricket jumper over his football tracksuit declaring his love for both English sports.

Harold Napier also loved regaling his charges with jokes, not always politically correct and very rarely raising more than a regulation titter from the boys.

Mr Napier handled George with particular care, spotting the passion and the talent, challenging the rebellious youth as well as encouraging him, building a relationship of trust. He wasn't intrusive, never prying to know more about the home life that any teacher would know lay at the root of George's refusal to conform to control. "Lawson" became "George" over time as the relationship grew and strengthened. George developed a deeper understanding of the skills and nuances of the game, not only his own fancy footwork but the ability to "read" the game, practice peppered with stories and insights from the weathered old pro. At Aveley, thanks to the. care and attention of the friendship and mentoring of Harold Napier, George grew a lifelong love of football

His skill matured to a point where, very soon, he was playing for his school year team and, later, for teams of years older than him. Success brought with it the most precious feeling of rising self-esteem . "I am *somebody!*" George could feel, without the reckless and rude behaviour he adopted off the pitch.

George was soon playing representative football for the district team and, when Harold Napier put him forward for a County trial, he earned a place on one of the youth teams without breaking sweat.

Success is addictive. With scant comfort at home, football took up all of George's attention and all his affection. And success continued to flow, with scouts from big, professional clubs taking an interest. Serious men from West Ham, Arsenal, Tottenham, all turned up to see him strut his stuff.

At fourteen, George chose to go with Millwall, lower down the league than the big boys; he didn't feel he was good enough for the top flight. The other clubs persisted, approaching George's father to sign him up. Frank sent them packing. Millwall had approached George directly and his father knew nothing about the invitation for George to attend trials. The club would pay his travel expenses and the trials were during the school holidays; his father need never know.

"It can take anything from six months to a year before we decide to take you on as an apprentice," one of the coaches cautioned the boys. Barely two weeks later, George stood before Benny Fenton, the manager of the famous docklands club.

"You want to play for Scotland one day?" Benny asked George.

"If I'm good enough," George replied.

"Right answer, lad," the manager said with a smile. He handed George the forms for joining the club as a Schoolboy Apprentice. "You'll have to get your father to sign them because you're under eighteen."

Frank Lawson had not shown any interest in George's passion for football, or anything else for that matter, never attended any of his games or asked about his progress. He refused to sign the forms. "It's not the life I have in mind for you," Frank said. "It's not a proper trade, a career for life." George forged his father's name on the papers anyway and attended the training sessions in secret.

Every Tuesday and Thursday, Mr Napier arranged for George to leave school early to get to Millwall on time. He also got lucky: he had chosen afternoon violin lessons to get out of more demanding studies and it turned out the music teacher lived close to the Millwall ground. George could sometimes get a lift just two tube stops away, a relief from the long journeys by bus and train and tube, especially in the dark of winter. There were no lifts on the way home, of course, no one even to meet him at the station. Neither Frank nor Lena even noticed his regular late coming home from school on training days.

George's special skills shone above those of the other schoolboy apprentices. The coach invited him to join in the training sessions with full team players. "You need to get used to this," he told the lad, awestruck to be training with legends and heroes like Derek Posey.

Just as everything was going well, George scuppered progress – perhaps patterned like his father, Frank. He had taken to pilfering from the other boys' kit for items he needed but could not afford, or ask his parents; they knew nothing of his secret training. He reasoned that the other lads had parents who would easily replace the stolen stuff, the same self-serving rationale that suited him so well in his daily life. The other lads reported the missing items and it didn't take long for suspicion to point to George and his habit of finding reasons to visit the changing rooms when the rest of the squad was out on the pitch.

Eager to help a player who showed such promise, the coach and staff offered to speak with George's parents. Out of the question. George walked away from the club and any chance of a professional football career. Boys he had trained with, like Jeff Pike and Paul Allen, went on to become highly successful footballers; George foisted his failure on parents who didn't give him the support his peers received. He was not yet inclined to take responsibility for his own misdemeanour, blame being the balm that patched up his pride.

Only Lena turned up to watch him play, just the once, in an amateur league game at Grays Football Club. She shouted and screamed from the stands, drunk and out of order as usual. George slunk away from the pitch, praying she may have gone off with some man by the time he came out of the changing room.

Saturday job

As soon as employment law would allow, George got a Saturday job working at at a butcher's shop in Aveley. He also worked in the butchery department of the local Co-op store. He now had money to buy the things he would otherwise have stolen and his pilfering impulse was quietened, if not altogether purged. He stole out of habit now, not always for lack of money. If he wanted a thing, he took it, stealing from shops, doorsteps, sheds, washing lines, and he was good at doing it undetected. His parents never bothered to ask where he got the clothes and shoes and colognes.

He joined the local youth club with Francis, learned to dance, chat to girls, dressed for the part and the parties with his own money.

It had always been a George-Francis double act, because the boys were so close together in age. Kenneth wasn't part of their adventures. He also couldn't enjoy having the support of a brother at school, as George did. At primary school, Kenneth was just starting out as George was getting ready to leave for secondary school, amongst the oldest boys. At secondary school, George was too concerned for his own swaggering status to be associating with his younger sibling. This distance between Kenneth and George would never quite ever be closed, however much affection and love they felt for each other.

Gregarious Jack-the-lad, popular with his peers and playmates, George remained a loner, avoiding the emotional closeness of a true friendship. One schoolmate was favoured with regular visits, but only because George loved the thick buttery toast on offer from the novelty of an electric pop-up toaster. Anyone getting too close might get to see the sad and succourless home life George suffered. He did not ever again want to become the subject of special attention, pity or ridicule.

At his father's Social Club, the older Lawson lads discovered table-tennis. George became quite good at it. The boys found an old table, in its two halves, lying dust-covered in a corner of the shed at the club. With an almost automatic reflex, they decided to steal it.

One dark morning, in the quiet early hours, Francis and George borrowed a wheelbarrow from their father's gardening shed and wheeled it across to the club. Pushing the barrow back, across the soft ground of sports pitches, was harder work and took longer than the lads had planned. They made it home unobserved just as the neighbourhood was stirring with those working early shifts.

They concealed the table on a concreted corner behind their garden, where neither neighbours nor parents would see it. But the corner was cramped and left little room for the fast, free arm smashes favoured by George – the bat would smash against a wall on the backswing. It was also a windy corner, the light ping pong ball often uncontrollable and just blown away. They played only a few games on the purloined table before away in their own shed – where Frank would likely never see it, anyway.

The gang

Before long, George was stealing things to sell on. He broke into his school at night to steal copper piping, smashed into a local shop to grab lighters and watches and anything else sellable he could carry away. Inevitably, his sideline put him into contact with others flirting with felony and George became the swaggering member of a gang that dealt in anything and everything.

The gang brought George a sense of belonging and status as he strutted about the streets of East London on frequent trips "up the Smoke" with them, splashing his cash on the latest reggae records, a favourite with some of the "skinheads" amongst the gang.

The gang also brought him to the attention of the local police.

One evening, George was all kitted up and ready to go on the pitch for a school football match when his father cycled right up to the touchline. Frank *never* came near any game George played.

"You're coming with me," Frank said, stern and concerned. "Right now."

Still in his football kit, George sat astride the crossbar of the bicycle as Frank pedalled home over the grass and gravel. A policeman was waiting in the parlour, wanting to question him about some stolen property. Remarkably, Frank held his temper as he escorted George to the police station for a formal caution. Perhaps he thought the caution might suffice, or after prison he felt in no position to preach about lawbreaking.

Most likely, he just didn't care – any more than did George. His brush with the law just served to boosted his standing with the bad boys.

Lena leaves

Just as life seemed to be ticking by, tickets-boo, everything changed.

Preparing for bed one night, George heard sobbing coming from his father's bedroom. He went in to see Frank sitting on the edge of his bed, face buried in his hands. He looked up to see George and broke into bawling.

"She's gone, George!" He wailed. "Your Mum has left us."

It didn't make sense to George. His father had been fairly well behaved since he returned from prison, drinking a lot less and not displaying any of the anger and violence that had driven Lena away before. George began to feel some sympathy for his father – and a growing resentment of his mother, who was surely the cause of the latest in a long line of leavings.

It didn't help that she had moved in with a man just up the road, whose son was in the same year as George at school. His mum being out of reach, George began to vent his frustration on her lover's boy. He abused and taunted the boy at every opportunity until he escalated to breaking a raw egg over the boy's head. Instantly, George experienced the same sense of shame he had when he had hit the girl at primary school, because violence was simply not in the nature of the youth who had seen so much of it as a child. He apologised profusely, helped the boy clean up, and they continued a more comfortable relationship.

George saw little of Lena once she had moved in with her new lover, and he cared for her even less; to his mind (as with so many today

...emn alcoholism), drinking was a choice Lena made. Even now, ...w understand it to be the mental illness it is, often caused by emotional turbulence and trauma at an early age. George blamed his mother and the ice began to form around the extravagant emotions he had once poured to her.

Lena had managed to snag a well-paid job. For all his disdain of her drinking and debauchery, George had no qualms about visiting her to tap her for some money. While he was there and even when he was leaving, there was never any exchange of affection or warmth.

"Give us a kiss!" Lena would lean to George at the door, but he couldn't bring himself to be close to the booze-ravaged face whose beauty had burned so deep in his heart as a boy. He would just turn and walk away, waving from the gate; Lena would blow him the kiss instead.

Life without Lena

Frank tried to keep things together, going to work and providing the essentials for the boys. He started to drink heavily again, however, and the frustrations and fears often overflowed into physical fury. As before, the slightest trigger could unleash an explosion.

Once, when George picked up a slab of butter to scrape some and spread on his potatoes, Frank lost control because he felt George was using too much. He grabbed the slab from George and tried to make him eat the entire half pound, pressing it into his face. He hadn't reckoned on George, now a street-hardened fifteen year old, standing up for himself. George challenged his father to a fist-fight. His father backed down and was even more a broken man in George's company from that day.

George saw this as a sign of weakness and became ever more cocky and careless in his behaviour, defiantly smoking in front of his father, for example, something he would never have dared to do before the showdown. He truanted from school whenever he pleased, knowing his father would never give him a hard time. He spent more and more time with his gang.

As soon as he was sixteen and legally allowed to do it, he left school altogether and found full time work, just as Francis had done.

Frank did the opposite; he left his comfortable job at Thames Board Mills, where he lad moved from the production line to the union office and announced that he was moving back to Dunoon. His mother was unwell and needed him to look after her; that was the formal reason, although being around daily evidence of Lena's alienated affections had worn him down. Both Francis and George turned down his offer to go with him, so he took Kenneth – heightening his alienation from his brothers – and headed back to Scotland without the older boys.

George was now settled in his job in London, in the freight forwarding office of a shipping company. He travelled down by train every day with Francis, who worked in Spitalfields Market. The two older brothers bonded ever closer, Kenneth even more out of the loop.

Frank found lodgings for Francis and George with Jock, a friend from the social club, and his wife. It was a full house, with Jock's brother also staying with them while he worked locally as an engineer. With no children of his own, Jock took care of his lodgers with an almost parental concern and affection. For the parentless boys, it was a contented and settled home for the first time in years.

They shared a double bed in the master bedroom, but that was hardly a bother to the Lawson lads. It was a haven they enjoyed after their work and social whirl, especially Sunday evenings, when they would religiously follow the latest charts on *Top of the Pops*.

Being Lawson children, they found time to go carousing as well. Staggering home in the early hours one morning, George holding Francis steady, the older boy said he smelled smoke in the air as they passed a local pub. George laughed it off. "Most likely just steam from the dishwasher," he pronounced.

Walking to the station with Francis the next morning, they saw that the pub had been entirely burnt to the ground during the night.

Danielle

George met Danielle in a pub, not surprisingly, in Aveley. The attraction was mutual and, as they got chatting, George was pleased to learn she came from South Ockendon, a nearby village.

Close enough to visit, but South Ockendon was "owned" by a rival gang to the one George ran with in Aveley. He drew back from calling on Danielle three times before he risked the trip. He rarely spent time with his Aveley crew now that he was working, but gangs have long memories..

Danielle and George began to meet regularly, to "go out." The smart, confident and courteous George also earned the approval of Danielle's parents.

At work, George was displaying the same traits as his father. Just when everything seemed to be sailing smoothly to success, George would find a way to withdraw and walk away. As with football, so with his daily crust.

For no particular reason that he would recall, he quit his job at the freight forwarding office for one at The Stock Exchange. It was a time of near-full employment and there was plenty of work about in the Square Mile for bright young men from Essex, with their easy access to Liverpool Street and Fenchurch Street.

Starting at the bottom as a messenger, as so many Essex lads before and since, George planned to work his way up to the trading floor where he could make buckets of his beloved money. He stuck at it for two years before abandoning that ambition.

His headstrong and impulsive attitude also led him to turn down another chance to follow his first dream, to play football for a living.

One of George's managers at The Stock Exchange served on the Board of Leyton Orient Football Club. Word of George's prowess had reached most of the clubs that mattered, scouts networking and comparing notes. The manager recognised George's name one day as he was handing out the post and offered him a try-out for the Orient squad. Stubborn George politely refused, partly because he shied away from closeness, not wanting to be beholden to anyone.

Dodgy dealing

Dating Danielle and pubbing with Francis still left plenty of time for George to see his gang. Drugs were now a big part of their scene, for personal use as well as dealing for the huge cash profit they produced.

He began to spend more time with them, dossing and dealing daily. Before long, he quit the job at The Stock Exchange to devote himself to making money on the wild side. It was a life he knew only too well and he slipped easily into the gang; despite its feuds and fights and friendships, it was a place where he belonged, where he had a status, not just another anonymous ant hustling in the City hive.

The gang was moving from petty theft and dealing to burglary. For George, this was a seminal moment. Breaking into other people's homes was a whole big step away from the pilfering and lifting he had ever entertained. When the gang entered the home of the grandmother of one member, George went along until he saw the rest of the boys picking up things and putting them into bags. They were burgling the family of one of their own! George protested he wanted no part of it and was told to leave, stand at the top of the road as a lookout for police or grandma returning home.

The police didn't take long to work out who had committed the burglary; the gang wasn't smart enough to pick a stranger as their victim, for a start. And it didn't take long for George to realise that the idea of any honour amongst thieves is mostly a myth. Others in the gang "grassed." Eventually every member was charged, even George was implicated by other gangers to spare their own likely sentences. George was arrested and bailed for a burglary in which he had no part at all.

The experience of police custody and the process of a criminal trial were of an entirely different order to anything George had endured before. His first inkling of the gravity was being locked in a holding cell during a court adjournment, not allowed to pop down the road for a quick pint. The seriousness soon hit when he heard himself being sentenced to three months in a Detention Centre.

Detention

Handcuffed to two police officers, George was taken by taxi from Chelmsford County Court to the detention centre in Oxfordshire – oddly, not too far from his first separation from familiar comforts, the foster care with Peggy when he was a tot. The taxi ride was light-hearted and easy-going and George began to feel that being "banged-up" would not be too bad.

The smugness disappeared as soon as they arrived at their destination.

The grim building loomed ominously in the evening half-light, the only habitation for miles around. The grim-faced and taciturn staff watched sternly as the officers signed the papers, unlocked the cuffs and handed George over. No words or pleasantries exchanged, just the bare minimum needed to get the transfer done, briskly and brusquely.

From the very start, any idea of comfort or consolation disappeared from George's mind. Perhaps as an innate defence to the horrors at home, he had developed a keen sensitivity to "atmosphere," a change in emotional energy around him. This sensitivity would later be integral to his development as a medium, but right now it just filled him with utter dread.

This was going to be different. This was going to be tough.

The Detention Centre was run like a "boot camp," with military precision and with the inmates kept constantly busy, harried, hard worked. Each day was punctuated by the staccato rhythm of orders barked at him: "Stand there;" "Take off those clothes;" "Get into the bath;" "Get out of the bath;" "Silence in the ranks!"

The very first order was to run at the double to a room where there stood a tin bath with about three inches of tepid water. "Get washed and get dressed in just your underwear," he was commanded. "Now take your clothes to the office and get your kit – run!"

The smart jumper and snazzy shirt, the new shoes, all were stuffed into a cardboard box and thrust up on a shelf with other boxes, as George put on the grey regulation top and trousers. He was nudged at a run down a painted-brick corridor to his cell, prodded to go in, and the heavy steel door thudded shut.

This was worse, in its way, than his last three-month stay in Oxford. This time, he was completely alone, not even his siblings there to share the complete isolation and humiliation. And he was old enough to think about all the dimensions of his predicament. George dissolved in tears of fear and self-pity. When he quietened, he resolved not to give in to tears again during his detention. Strong willed as he remains to this day, he kept his promise throughout his sentence.

Every trace of his life outside would be stripped from George, from the orders that challenged his normal do-as-I-please behaviour to his appearance. Like many of his inmates, George had a fashionably long hair style. On the very first day, he was lined up with other inmates as, one by one, they entered a room from which, later, they emerged with identical, close-cropped hair cuts.

One or two emerged holding their noses, spots of blood splatter peeking through fingers.

"What happened to you?" George asked one lad.

"I forgot to say 'Sir!' when I spoke," the boy replied.

George didn't make the same mistake when officers harangued him during his haircut, firing questions up close to his face. He didn't get his nose punched, but they pulled painfully on his sideburns before they were shaved and tugged at the hairs in his armpit. George was savvy enough to see they were trying to provoke him into a punishable reaction. He didn't rise to it, but the point was made: the officers were in charge, could treat him as they pleased, and he was powerless against them.

George had always challenged and thwarted authority. Authority was biting back, big time. He watched as other inmates tried to play the "hard man" game with the officers, trying to make kudos from spending time in solitary, but he kept his behaviour in check. George toeing the line was in its way, albeit dimly, a beginning of accepting consequences and his own responsibility. But there was a long road still to travel before epiphany.

Dormitory days

George kept his nose clean and his behaviour modest, rewarded by a job in the kitchen. It meant less time locked up in his cell and the occasional extra tidbit from the refectory. Always good at work he enjoyed, George worked his way up to be second in command to the chef himself.

The position as second to the chef gave him the privilege of serving and clearing up in the officers' mess. Here, he could gather up the cigarette butts the officers left in the ashtrays, wrap them up in paper and sneak them back to his cell. Tobacco was tantamount to gold dust and his cell mates would tear open the buts and make new cigarettes rolled up in newsprint or regulation-stiff toilet paper, using spit and sometimes diluted toothpaste to glue the ends together.

After four weeks in a single cell, George was moved to a dormitory with five other boys who worked in the kitchen with him. It took a few days to work out the dynamics of living with four other feisty fellows, but it helped that they worked together and soon settled into a steady co-existence. There wasn't much chance to do much else than sleep in the dorm; the boys had to speak in whispers after lights out, or suffer some sort of censure or punishment – losing the kitchen job would be hard. Worse, one inmate's offence would bring punishment to the entire dormitory cell, so each of the boys made sure the others didn't step out of line.

Daily bed and kit inspection was one example of this "collective responsibility." If one lad's bed was not made up to perfect specifications, all corners neatly tucked, all effects stowed away, the entire dorm would have to strip their beds and make them up again – at double quick time, to avoid penalties for being late for morning parade!

George's model behaviour slipped only twice. The first time was when a he was attacked by a smart-arse who had been taunting and goading him for days. George had ignored the provocation until the boy lunged at him with a plastic knife, in a quiet corner out of sight of any officers. The plastic snapped impotently on George's taut belly, but George swung a fast fist in the fool's face, connecting on the nose and drawing blood. An officer turned the corner just as the boy was getting up.

"What's going on here, then?" The officer asked, seeing the bloodied nose and the broken knife on the floor. Neither admitted anything untoward. "Tripped and hit my nose on the floor, sir," the other lad replied. "That's right, sir," George agreed. Unconvinced, but with no evidence or complaint, the officer ordered both boys to clean the dining room floor with a toothbrush. Both boys breathed a sigh of relief and escaping the worst punishment – time added to their detention.

Similar mocking was directed at George by the lad who worked the "pig bins" in the kitchen. He used every chance to torment George with smart remarks and taunts. After weeks of taking it, it was the thought of being belittled amongst his peers that finally made George snap. He grabbed one of the heavy metal trays from the drying racks and swung it with full force at the pig-bin boy, knocking him off his feet, winded. The kitchen was not a place the short-staffed officers bothered to monitor and George escaped unpunished and unblemished.

Both incidents repeated the now familiar pattern of George's behaviour: a sudden and violent explosion of fury, followed by remorse at what he had inflicted on another. Violence was not a pleasure for George and his own disturbed him almost as much as what he had witnessed with his father.

George had no trouble with the physical exertions of detention. He got to enjoy working in the gym, somersaulting on the vaulting horse with ease and delight, relishing the soaring and swinging of the parallel bars. The love of physical fitness would remain with George in the years ahead, bolstered by his lifelong passion for football.

Mum visits

Lena had eventually learned, probably over a bar counter somewhere, about George's detention – he hadn't mentioned his court appearance and no one he knew had been there to hear his sentence. Somehow in her stupor, maybe again with the help of some drinking pal, she had navigated the labyrinth of the justice system and tracked him down to the detention centre.

George wished she hadn't bothered.

She was, of course, in the blackout drunk stage – fully functioning, but out of her mind. She took out a pack of sandwiches and offered him one. Eating was strictly forbidden during visiting times – anything other than talking was forbidden, even hugs other than the briefest at meeting and leaving. The officers immediately confiscated the sandwich and firmly escorted Lena from the room; visiting time was over.

George was happy that it was the only time Lena bothered to come.

Good behaviour earned him remission and he was released eight weeks and two days after he was first checked into the detention centre. Only his old street clothes didn't fit quite as comfortably as they had when he had handed them over in the box. Exercise and physical work, with access to good regular meals (and extra portions) had built up muscle and bulk.

The clothes were stiff and dry from storage, chafing and pinching at all the joints; not quite the casual swagger George had imagined. With the wages he had gathered from his kitchen work in his pocket, he made his way to Paddington, then Fenchurch Street and, finally, Purfleet.

Danielle was waiting for him, the first time anyone had ever welcomed him home. He wasn't sure if the same would be true of Jock, if there was even a home for him to return to.

His worries vanished the instant Jock greeted him with a big smile and arms opened wide. In a life mostly devoid of kindness and care,

Jock was a selfless exception, showing all the support and understanding entirely missing from his parents. He treated George and Francis for all intents and purposes as a grandfather might, or an older uncle. They felt like family.

Football figured again in George's life during this settled time with Jock. He was encouraged and cajoled to join the local Sunday League by another George, Mr Bishop, who managed the team. Encouraged by Mr Bishop and mentored by the coach, George enjoyed playing again. As he improved, so did the team, regularly reaching the Sunday League Cup Final.

Jock's wife's disability was uncomfortable for George, especially at meal times, when Jock had to spoon feed her like a baby. As she grew worse, George finally decided to move out. Francis decided to stay on. It was the beginning of a drifting apart that grew wider with time.

George moved in with his mother and her lover, sharing a bedroom with the boy on whose head he had once broken an egg. The move soon proved to be a mistake. Lena was still drinking all day, while her lover was at work, and he would start drinking as soon as he got home. The arguments were a reprise of what George had witnessed every day with his father. As with Frank, the lover's fury developed into physical violence at anyone or anything within fist reach. George packed his bags and walked out of the unkempt and dismal house.

He turned up at Danielle's door and his parents allowed him to stay with them until he found a place to rent nearby. A workmate put him in touch with a lady who had a spare room in a block of flats nearby. She had a couple of dogs and George the animal lover soon felt right at home.

Dissolution days

Without the moderating attention of Danielle's parents, he soon slipped back into the company of the the unsavoury characters that had led him to detention. The weeks and months that followed drifted past in a haze of drugs and dealing and all-night raves, long weekends of non-stop drink, drugs, dancing and dossing.

Once, he followed a crowd he had met at a festival into London, out of his tree for days before he ran out of money for the drugs, got bored and headed back home.

From the snappy smartness of earlier times, George began to look like a hippie, long hair, hairy face and regulation Afghan coat – the very type his old skinhead mates would have targeted. On the tube one Cup Final day, a crowd of close-cropped Newcastle supporters did just that: chased him across platforms and tunnels before he escaped, by jumping on a departing train just as the doors closed.

The dissolute lifestyle was funded, as ever, by pilfering. As he had at Millwall, George began to steal even from his Sunday League team-mates. Anything he could sell for money was fair game.

As with Millwall, it didn't take long for suspicion to fall firmly on the likely lad, Lawson. Never directly accused, and playing pretty poorly anyway because of his lifestyle, George decide to walk away from football. Again.

Kenneth came back from Scotland, Nan Lawson having passed away – news no one had passed to George until he heard it from Kenneth. Their father stayed on, sending Kenneth down alone. He was staying at Lena's home because Jock's wife was in too poor a shape for him to look after a fifteen-year old boy, Francis busy with work and his own romantic relationship.

George again rebuffed Kenneth, who somehow sought him out and wanted to follow his big brother around. Eighteen-year old George had no more time for his little brother at this time than he had back in school days. Patterns and dynamics in relationships have an extraordinary durability.

Doting Danielle

Danielle's devotion to George remained steady and unwavering throughout these days of drugs and disappearances.

She would often dutifully tag along to some of his jaunts, there to make sure he was safe, patiently seeing him home without a word of reproach. Eventually, her tenderness, support and constancy helped him to climb out of the decadent daze.

As his mind cleared, George heard his heart. With a start, he realised that he was in love, for the first time in his life. He loved Danielle and wanted to spend his life with her. He knew also that he would have to find a regular job to stand any chance of realising the new dream.

He got work as a labourer with a local building contractor and saved up the £60 needed for a marriage licence. Danielle and George were married at South Ockendon Catholic Church in 1976 and moved in with Danielle's parents. Just as he had when he lodged with them, George fitted in with the family perfectly well and this was a settled and contented time.

After a while with the builder, George found work on the assembly line of the Ford Tractor Plant in West Thurrock. It was better money and more reliable than the seasonal ups and downs of the building trade. The work was monotonous and boring, stencilling cases all day long, but George enjoyed the camaraderie of his own coterie of pranksters – schoolyard habits – who became known as "The Dirty Dozen."

And football found him again.

The man

Football and fatherhood

Football at the top level is a small community, coaches and scouts moving about, networking and sharing news about likely lads. The manager of East Tilbury Football Club, lower in the leagues than the clubs that had once feted George, had heard of the Lawson lad and seen him play in the Sunday League finals.

He approached George to play for the club. George's first reaction was to reject the invitation, but the manager knocked on his door one Sunday morning because a virus had left his team short of key players.

"Just this once, George," he pleaded. "We're desperate."

George agreed and thoroughly enjoyed having the ball at his feet once again. He agreed to play regularly and life settled into a comfortable rhythm of domestic contentment, regular work and Sunday football. George felt like one of the "normal" people, for once in his life. The couple moved out of the family home into a council flat, when their names reached the top of the list.

The prescribed portrait of working class prosperity was completed when George and Danielle, both with steady money and modest lifestyles, had saved up enough money for a deposit to buy their own home. They were the proud owners of the very first house on a new development, close to Tilbury Power Station.

In July, 1979, three years into their marriage and as steady as a couple could be, Danielle delivered their son, William. The boy seemed to be the cherry on the cake of their cosy and conventional life. George doted on his boy, trying to be the father he wished Frank had been.

It would soon turn out to be the toughest test, as George was required to shoulder the weight of being stereotype of sole breadwinner, man of the house and all the other pressures and expectations of that role. A testing time for most first time fathers, George made an effort to improve life for his family. He enrolled at the local college to earn his GCE certification, improving his chances of moving up in the Ford hierarchy. Life on a single income was tight, but they managed – until a strike slashed even that income to subsistence level.

When the going got tough, George generally got going – out of the door. He stuck stoically at the role of stalwart provider for a while, but the mortgage, the bawling baby, his wife's silent suffering, later undisguised reproach, all became an overwhelming, oppressive environment whenever he was at home. He spent an increasing amount of time on football, training, playing, even touring Holland and Spain with the squad. Most of his spare time was spent hanging out with his mates, usually getting drunk. Losing his licence for driving while drunk was inevitable and served only to deepen the dissatisfaction.

Farewell to Ford

George gave up his job at Ford, saying he would attend college full time to get the qualifications for a better job. Danielle decided she could do better fending for William and herself without the worry and wrangling; four years into the marriage, she asked George to leave.

Fatherhood for George had been a fleeting year when he barely spent any time with his boy, an echo of his own childhood. For a brief period after he was expelled, George perhaps saw more of his son than when he had lived under the same roof. He visited the boy every other week until the divorce was finalised, the dutiful dad, but these visits trickled to none until he lost touch with Danielle and William completely.

Like father, like son, George had as little empathy or care for little William as had Frank Lawson for his boys.

News of Danielle remarrying, selling the house to move in with her new husband, still didn't spur George into renewing his relationship with his son, to lay claim to his "blood". He did show intense interest when Danielle applied to change William's surname to that of his step-father, but not through any care for the boy who had barely known him as a father. He protested furiously to Social Services, self-serving arguments denying the reality that he had stopped caring about the boy barely months after his birth. William's name change was ratified and George's son no longer uses the Lawson name.

Moving, moving on

After a brief spell living with a football friend and another marooned and motorless miles from mates in East Tilbury, George eventually settled with another friend in Grays. They got on well and being minutes from college made it easier to continue with his "A" levels. Income from a paid position with the Students Union boosted his benefits, paying the rent with some spare for student socialising.

George completed his "A" levels in History and English Literature. Enjoying the success and enthused with educating himself, he enrolled for a three-year degree in law at North East London Polytechnic.

He left his mate's flat in Grays to be closer close to his new place of learning. At first, he shared a house with a group of rowdy and untidy students just out of Sixth Form College, before finding a room with another student his own age, who lived in a house by himself. The top floor of a three-storey town house seemed perfect at first, but his new landlord was fond of drinking – every evening.

Coming home drunk most evenings, he would noisily try to cook himself a fry up. He used gas and George was concerned for his safety in case of fire; he made careful plans for escape, just in case. This, too, was a brief stay. His next lodgings, with a comfortable family close to college, served him well enough and he stayed for a year.

There was the brief, obligatory college fling. George enjoyed the attentions of a student nurse, with a kindness and caring typical of her chosen profession. George was unable to return her devotion and found a typically thoughtless way to finish the friendship before it developed into deeper commitment. He was still playing football with East Tilbury and the club was booked for a tour of Spain. His girlfriend didn't want him to go and George told her he wouldn't; on the morning the squad was leaving, he telephoned her from the airport to tell her he was off!

The second year of a degree course is when the hard work begins; the first year is fairly free and easy. George soon found the rigorous demands cramping his freedom, losing interest and losing sight of any long-term goal. He dropped out and frittered away his student grant.

Football came to the rescue in a different way. One of the managers at East Tilbury Football Club arranged an interview for George with the insurance company where he was a senior executive. George got the job, collecting premiums from door to door. It was a well paid job and George was entrusted with large amounts of cash – how premiums were paid on the doorstep – correctly recording and safely banking the payments.

"Give it large". George succumbed to the inevitable temptation, dipping into the collections to fund his fondness for fun and frolic. Following in father Frank's footsteps, he got the sack.

Liz

Now twenty-nine years old, George was earning good money as ship's chandler at Tilbury Docks, after a year working on refurbishing ships. He was lodging with a friend and his wife, who had a young baby; being part of the contented family added to George's sense of feeling that life was settling down.

Liz was the hairdresser at a salon that had a discount offer on Thursday evenings. Ever eager for a bargain, George spotted Liz on his first visit and recognised her as a girl who had caught his eye several times in a local wine bar. A haircut goes with a good chat and George warmed to the girl, but could not summon up the nerve to suggest a date.

Liz had no such compunctions, approaching him in a wine bar that both had come to with their own crowd of friends. "Are you walking me home, or what?" She asked, with a cheeky smile.

He walked her home and the next day borrowed his friends' Vauxhall Mantra to take Liz on their first date, a trip to London's West End. George felt at ease with Liz as he showed her around Soho and Trafalgar Square and the theatre district.

They began "going steady," marred only by a very brief interruption by Danielle. She approached George, hinting they might get back together again for the sake of William, and he immediately sought out Liz to explain he had to do "the decent thing." Liz was very understanding, even when George returned a few days later to resume their romance;

Danielle had merely been using George as a ploy to push her partner into proposing marriage.

George moved out of lodgings, renting a house from a friend, and Liz began to spend most of her time with him instead of her own home. When this accommodation had to be vacated, Liz found George a room at her sister's and moved back in to live with her mother. The romance remained steady throughout, the couple meeting regularly at the local pub and out socialising with friends.

Skiathos

They went on holiday to Skiathos with friends and fell in love with the place. Like so many holidaymakers, they mused about living there. Unlike others, they decided to do something about it. Back home, they resigned from their jobs, booked basic accommodation and cheap one-way tickets to begin their grand adventure.

Both found work in local bars, fun in the evenings and with plenty of free time to enjoy the sun and sea. George's employer was an American from New Jersey who insisted on fraternising with his patrons with a vodka, finishing two whole bottles most nights. The fights with his wife that followed closing time were hardly a new experience for George!

Life was good on the island for a good few months before the familiar restlessness reared up for George. Whenever things were "on a roll," his familiar pattern soon led him away from the straight road.

He began to socialise with a vengeance, drinking prodigiously, often disappearing for days on end on a bender. Liz, patient as ever, tolerated the reckless disregard for a full eighteen months, before deciding she had enough. She returned to Essex in Christmas 1988, alone. Four months later, fed up with the slow season and struggling for spare spending money, George returned home as well.

Liz, living with her mother and now working for a local conservatory company, agreed to give their relationship another chance. George found a room with a friend in Grays, found a job as assistant transport manager for a logistics company, and life returned to an even keel. The couple, both with good regular income, eventually bought a house they would call home for the next sixteen years.

George's careless attitude did not change. Once, when a house a few doors down caught fire and he had to evacuate his own, George was enjoying a pint in the pub when Liz burst in, close to tears. At first, not able to enter the street because of the fire brigade cordon, she had feared for George. Neighbours soon told her where to find him and she was furious at his devil-may-care attitude.

"What are you doing her?" Liz demanded to know. "Our house could be burning to the ground and all you can do is sixty here getting drunk!"

"What do you want me to do?" George said with a sardonic glance around at his pals. "I'm not a fireman."

Farewell, Lena and Frank

Francis broke the news to George in a pub.

"Mum's dead," he told his younger brother.

"Oh, yeah?" George replied nonchalantly.

"You should come to the funeral," Francis advised. "Last chance to pay your respects, you won't get another."

All three brothers attended the cremation and Lena's surviving family, Nan Wilson, Uncle George and even Auntie Margaret came down for the ceremony. Frank Wilson remained in Dunoon - either he hadn't heard, or he didn't care. George felt no remorse or loss and there was no plaque to commemorate his mother after the event.

When Frank Lawson passed away in Dunoon, it was Kenneth who sought out George to give him the news. Kenneth did not manage to persuade his brother to attend the funeral of a father he had never respected in life.

Disregard for any "normal" rules of behaviour was part of George's nature. He got the sack from his job with the logistics company for fiddling his expenses. After a few jobless months, he found work with a freight forwarding company, on the strength of his knowledge of transport and logistics. He was sacked from this job, too, pilfering stock – and for his part in helping to set up a roadside robbery; nothing could be proved, so he escaped prosecution.

Jobs were easy enough to find back then. For George Frederick Lawson, they were just as easy to lose with his cavalier, self-serving character, and he rarely showed any concern or upset at being shown the door yet again. Long-suffering, loyal Liz kept the show on the road, working hard and steady to make sure the bills got paid.

As easy as slipping on slime, George drifted back into drugs, using and selling amphetamines and speed. The odd petty theft made up the pocket money for his party life. On a whim, he brought some bongos and joined up with a band doing local gigs and clubs, spending more and more time away from loving Liz. As ever, George was completely oblivious to the effect of his behaviour on Liz, or anyone else for that matter. It was the George Lawson show, all the way.

Liz even took out a loan to help settle money George owed to his local supplier for a drug delivery that went wrong. He was attacked and robbed by the gang to whom he was delivering and, though his own gang later recovered most of the haul, he was obliged to pay for what was lost.

George took Liz's kindness and generosity as no more than his due and his descent into dissolution continued. By 1997, he had moved on from amphetamines and speed to selling and using cocaine.

The Law

They may take their time, but the police usually find their man., and they found George with a stash of drugs after watching his activities for some time.

He was grabbed at a service station on the A12, by three police cars boxing him in. He tried to swallow his booty but an officer smashed the driver window and hauled him out before he could ingest the evidence. He was taken to then-new police station in Witham and appeared at Chelmsford County Court on Monday, where he was bailed.

The prospect of prison didn't slow George one bit. Instead, he embarked on an even more frenetic crime spree to build up a nest egg for when he was released. Thought of providing for Lena didn't figure in his concerns. He was reckless now and was arrested and charged with other offences while on bail, utterly unconcerned that his time inside might be prolonged.

He was convicted for "possession with intent to supply" and sentenced to a four years in prison, with a minimum of two years before he might be eligible for parole. It was March 1999. Forty-four year old George would attend court again while in prison, for offences he had committed while on bail, pleading guilty on advice from the judge who had sentenced him in the first place, so that any new sentence would run concurrently and not add more time.

He faced the prospect of serving time in Chelmsford Prison, focused only on himself and what he faced, without any thought of the world outside. He barely dwelt on Liz and the ordeal she would also be facing, paying the bills and mortgage, facing the shame of her partner being a convicted criminal. Liz continued to support him, with letters and regular visits despite her work and chores; George simply took this for granted as right and due.

The insular, self-protecting and self-serving shell built around his spirit as a child remained closed to anything other than his own comfort. The child truly is father to the man.

Chelmsford Prison

If he had imagined prison might be like the detention experience of his youth, George was soon disabused of the notion during induction week.

Even today, new prisoners are locked up in their cell during induction for twenty-four hours a day, released for just one hour of exercise. At Chelmsford Prison, this was split into a half hour in the morning and another half hour in the evening. You left your cell for the odd assessment or class, but even meals were delivered to your cell. Locked up on a Friday, George didn't get his induction assessment until the following Monday, when he was allocated to a wing.

Most of his early days were spent in a daze, his brain still soaked with the daily dose of drugs and drink. He was assessed for drug addiction and offered a place on the rehab wing, but didn't feel inclined to be locked up in a cell with recovering addicts. His own dependence was not so bad, he reasoned, and opted for a cell in a drug-free wing, where there was no alternative but cold turkey.

He did encounter inmates with a drug addiction during his time at Her Majesty's Pleasure, saw how desperate they seemed and began to understand the impact of his own dealing. Addiction, once it takes a grip, in *not* a conscious lifestyle choice, the view he had taken to clear his own conscience. He resolved never to have anything to do with drugs again, once he got clean in prison; it was not a resolution he could keep once he was out.

Even on the wing, you spent all your time locked up in your cell unless you have a job. Jobs are scarce, especially for newcomers – most of the plum positions already belong to long-term inmates and "trustee" prisoners. You went to the refectory for your food, a brief outing because you brought it back to your cell to eat, with your cell mates. Being on a wing also allowed "association," time out of the cell when you could mingle freely with other prisoners – as freely as the watching wardens would allow.

George spent the locked up hours getting to grips with routine tasks like laundry, letters, visiting conditions and ordering "canteen," your regular delivery of personal delights such as tobacco, sweets, special soap and so on. You ordered your canteen at the beginning of the week and got it towards the end, Thursday or Friday. Canteen day was a high point of every week, a hive of activity as prisoners settled any "swaps" borrowed from other inmates. You could only order canteen if you had money in your prison spending account, either paid in by someone outside or earned by working on a prison job. Neither option was open to George and his prime priority was to get himself a job.

To start with, George opted for a "bed watch" cell because it meant sharing with only one other prisoner. His cellmate was considered a suicide risk because he was not taking well to his imprisonment. The unlikeliest men seemed to be badly affected by the experience of incarceration. George was required to keep an eye on his cellmate and alert officers is anything seemed amiss. George spent hours of their close confinement consoling and trying to divert his fellow prisoner, with little success.

George himself adjusted to prison life well, feeling comfortable with the regular meals, the routine and the security of officers on the lookout for any signs of threat or danger. Other inmates, generally the long-termers with little to lose, would occasionally lash out in frustration – either with other inmates for imagined insults or other transgressions, or with the officers – and end up with time in solitary confinement. This meant just a cardboard chair during the day, no other furniture or entertainment, and a bare mattress at night. George was determined never to suffer that punishment.

Riot and responsibility

Precious association time had been reduced because of staff shortages and, during one exercise period, prisoners staged a sit-in/lie-down protest, refusing to return to their cells. The Governor eventually addressed the convicts, assuring them they had made their point and association time would be restored.

George and most of the other prisoners were mollified and went back inside, but a hard core refused to budge. It was this band that rioted as darkness fell, the sound of shouting, banging and crashing reminding George of the battle scenes in the film *Zulu*.

All was quiet the next day. At association, George learned that the troublemakers had been whisked away during the night and relocated at widely dispersed prisons throughout the country.

George was relieved he had the good sense not to get involved. His focus on responsible behaviour drew the company of others like himself, intent on completing their sentences without trouble. The sense of belonging he had enjoyed with his gang mates on the outside was mirrored in prison. The company of the steady crowd helped him avoid the more troublesome characters and groups.

Three months free of drugs and alcohol, George retook the assessment test he had failed to complete during his hazy induction. He sailed through and was offered a job in the kitchen – work with which he was familiar from his detention days. Being out of the bed watch cell was relief enough, but his cellmate was also soon moved to another wing, so George now had a cell all to himself. Happy days!

He applied for gym time, to improve his fitness and at first could only use the facility at weekends. Once the gym staff got to know him and see he was serious about fitness, he was allowed gym time every other day. He also started to play football again.

Red band rewards

Education courses were actively encouraged; you could be excused work if you were needed in a class. George got stuck into training his mind as well.

His good behaviour was rewarded by being chosen for a privileged and prized "red band" job that only the Governor could authorise. He became a "Womble", a cleaner/litter picker, the nickname coming from the popular TV programme about creatures who collected litter on Wimbledon Common. Hardly glamorous work, but it meant a single occupancy cell whose door was left open all day. He could come and go as he pleased and more or less wander the wing as he willed, unsupervised.

Freedom almost always carries temptation and George was not one to resist an easy "score" when he felt he could get away with it. He was invited by other inmates to deliver packages from cell to cell, in return for goodies from their "canteen" – chocolates, a half ounce of tobacco, fruit juices, things he couldn't afford from his own meagre earnings.

Bucking the system had always been an essential element in George's need to assert himself, especially as he could see little danger of getting caught, no one watched him. He succumbed to the temptation and enjoyed the fruits of felony; for once, he was right in not being found out.

He pushed the limits further when he realised he could lay his hands easily on the ingredients for making hooch and began distilling. Security staff, who had already begun to have suspicions about George's delivery service, discovered some of his stash. They reported the matter to the Governor, along with their suspicions that it was George's doing. The Governor visited George in his trustee cell.

"Security are pretty sure you have something to do with this, George," the Governor said. "But there is no proof and it's hard to know what to do with you."

"I don't want the job anyway, if Security are going to be on my back all the time," George replied.

"What job *would* you want to do?"

George saw this as the moment to turn the situation, pushing his luck.

"I'd like to work in the gym," George demanded, adding: "And I want to be moved to Cat D."

He was currently classed as a Category C. Achieving "Cat D," Category D, meant eligibility to serve time in an open prison.

"Leave it with me," the Governor said.

Gym jobs were especially hard to come by, but George was released from wombling to work with a contractor that was refurbishing and redecoration the prison. The Governor was true to his word with his status; barely a year into his stretch at Chelmsford, George was awarded Category D stratus and applied for a transfer to an open prison.

The very week he started the gym job he had asked for, prison officers knocked on his cell door and told him to pack up his belongings. He was being transferred to Spring Hill open prison; security protocol prevented prisoners knowing of a transfer until the morning of the move.

Spring Hill

If George had enjoyed the privileges of being a trustee at Chelmsford, confinement at Spring Hill was altogether more convenient and comfortable.

He had his own hut, with a key to his own front door and the freedom to roam the grounds with no fences or barriers in the way. Open prisons are intended to help prisoners adjust to life in the world outside, but for George there was a strong impulse to just abscond. Some prisoners couldn't resist and *did* abscond, only to be re-arrested and put back into a secure prison, often with time added to their sentence.

For once, George did not give into his habitual behaviour. Being in Spring Hill itself was proof that keeping his nose clean yielded positive benefits. He couldn't resist the occasional breach of rules, to assure himself that he was no slave to authority and was free to do what suited *him* above all.

Good behaviour at Chelmsford probably helped also in getting George a job at Spring Hill right away, working in the gardens; eventually, prisoners might even earn the right to work outside the facility. Visiting times were more frequent and informal and Liz visited George regularly.

After twenty-eight days of good behaviour, he was eligible for home visits once a week. He would leave the prison at eight in the morning and had to be back inside by six. George made good use of this freedom – too good, on one occasion, because he spent the whole day getting drunk with his old reprobates. He was breathalysed on his return, judged to have broken the good behaviour code and denied home visits for a period of "lay down" of twenty-eight days.

George next secured a job working in the Officers' Mess, building a good rapport with the lady canteen manager. She seemed preoccupied with getting George to eat, eat all the time! George resisted, intent on building up his stamina and fitness and keeping up his programme of regular long runs.

He did love tuna and, when an opportunity presented itself, the chancer grabbed a big tin of the stuff and stashed it away in his hut. It was discovered during a snap inspection.

"Where did you get this?" asked the officer who had found it.

"The Officers' Mess," George answered. *I'm in trouble now,* he thought.

His cordial relationship with the canteen manager saved him: she told the investigating officer that she had given the tin to George, to feed him up because he never ate while he was at work. The fates had taken a hand again, saving George the ordeal of being shipped back to a secure prison immediately, and not Chelmsford, because that was the summary punishment for breaking open prison rules.

Lottery luck

To prepare for working on jobs outside the prison, Spring Hill inmates had to serve twelve weeks of voluntary work, ferried to and from by prison transport. George landed a placement at the local hospital, mostly photocopying and filing work – hardly inspiring, but being outside the prison precincts was a welcome relief. It was September 2001, the month of the Twin Towers attacks in New York.

On one of his days out, George visited a Post Office for some cigarettes and bought a lottery ticket with the spare change. When he checked his numbers that evening, without too much care or expectation, he noticed that he had four of the numbers for that draw. *That's a handy sixty-odd quid,* he thought to himself. When he took the ticket into the Post Office the next day, he learned that he had actually matched *five* numbers and won over £1,600!

Problem: no way could he take all that cash back to prison with him, because he shouldn't have bought the lottery tickets in the first place. The Post Office was able to issue cheques for the winnings, however, so George asked for a cheque £1,600 to be issued in Liz's name and pocketed the spare forty-odd pounds in cash.

The win was no windfall for Liz. George sent the cheque to her with a note asking her to use the money to buy, tax and insure a second-hand car for him, so he could have his own transport when he was offered more work outside the prison. Typically, there was no concern for helping Liz with the household bills.

When he had finished his voluntary twelve weeks and was ready for paid employment, as a labourer for a local building firm refurbishing a manor house, Liz brought the car to him at Spring Hill and returned home by train.

Lucky escapes

The urge to "duck and dive" was a reflex in the Lawson lad and temptation was never far away.

George had noticed that one of his fellow inmate workers on the building site, an affable enough chap, would disappear for long periods without any explanation. The man approached him one day, asking him to act as lookout while he attended to some "business."

George agreed, up to a point. He followed the inmate to the other side of woods surrounding the manor house, but then remembered his experience with the drug delivery that went wrong years ago. He refused to go to the place his mate was going to do his "business"

Within minutes of leaving George, the other inmate came running past him, shouting: "If anyone asks, you haven't seen me!" Another man came running up to George, asking if he had seen anyone running past. George pointed in the direction opposite to where he had seen his mate disappear into the woods, thinking he had saved his fellow inmate. The chap had, in fact, changed direction and was hiding in the very spot to which George pointed. He saw George pointing, however, and shifted position to escape discovery.

Sixth sense or some other influence spared George from disaster, as it did when he undertook a "vodka run."

Vodka was fifty pounds for a big bottle in the stores outside the prison. Inside, he was offered double that price if he could sneak the contraband into the compound. The risk if caught, as with any infraction of the regulations, would be whisking away to a secure prison and possible added time. George predictably decided to chance it.

He hid the bottle in a rucksack which he left in the boot of his car, which was always parked in a designated space outside the compound. After dark, he put on dark clothes and a mask, leaving one of his cell mates as lookout, with instructions to cough if there was any sign of a "screw" on the prowl.

The night was cold, wet and windy as he dodged the spotlights to his car, slung the bag back over his shoulders (bottle safely wrapped to avoid any clinking) and carefully made his way back.

Yards from his hut, he heard a cough. He dropped to the ground immediately – right into a deep, cold, muddy pothole. Laying as still as he could, he waited for some sign it was safe to surface. Ten long minutes passed without any signal before George had enough. He sprinted to his hut, hooded head down, as fast as he could – the gym work and running paid off. He made it to his hut without a hitch and hurriedly ducked inside. His lookout mate was sitting on George's bed without a care in the world.

"What happened?" George asked. "Why did you cough?"

"Wasn't me," his friend replied with a chuckle, seeing George soaked and soiled with mud. "One of the others was out having a fag. Must have been just as you got here."

If that wasn't unnerving enough, the vodka did its work and several inmates got prodigiously drunk, shouting and singing and falling about. George dreaded that loose lips might leak his name as the smuggler and was immensely relieved not to be found out. That was his first and last vodka run, but it was not his only ramble off the regulation road; George Lawson didn't live by any rules but his own. He saw several inmates sent back to secure prison for bucking the system, some "grassed" by others to save their own skin, but the Lawson drive to duck and dive didn't diminish.

Throughout the two years he served, dodging the demands of authority was George's internal strategy, to feel as if he was in charge of his own destiny, not some stupid system or stuck-up "screws." A lot of his time was spent planning and plotting, listening and learning about ways in which he could carry on his crime career when he got out. If prison is intended to reform offender, it failed utterly with George Frederick Lawson.

Seven hundred and thirty days after he entered the gates of Chelmsford Prison – sentences were expressed in days, not weeks or months – George was paroled and returned home to Liz. He was now forty-five years old.

Home discomforts

Many prisoners emerge from incarceration with a feeling of entitlement to empathy and understanding, as if the world outside needs to appreciate the ordeal they have been through. Even those who may accept their sentence as justly deserved feel that they have served their time and expect immediate absolution and acceptance.

The reality, of most folk being wary of associating with a jailbird, of being tainted as somehow untrustworthy, of finding steady work hard to come by, is entirely different from the happy homecoming they might have imagined in their incarceration. People have moved on with their lives, increasing the sense of being "left out." Many find it very hard to accept and the doubts can take years to dispel. George was typical of this entitlement mentality.

He spent most of his early days back at home in a rage. He raged at anything and everything that didn't go his way. He had developed an insularity in prison that amplified the feeling of isolation, his hallmark since boyhood. He stopped socialising, disliking crowds. Patient support from his parole officer, familiar with such difficulties, slowly settled George back into the rhythm and requirements of regular life.

He was offered three months of part-time work by a pal at a pallet-selling place, but the recklessness resurfaced as soon as that employment ended. He discovered the dubious joys of betting on horses, squandering the meagre money he earned without a penny to pay the mortgage and bills.

He took up playing bongos again, in a band and also busking on his own. Liz's frustration and worry at his feckless attitude made no difference. George was intent on resuming the road he had left when he had been locked up. To top up the pitiful income from banging bongos, he began dealing again with an old crony – and that was a straw too heavy for Liz to carry. She told him she had had enough and wanted him to leave.

For Liz, who had patiently and gently borne all the burden of being George's partner for years, this was not an easy thing to do. Even George, after initially pleading to save himself from the inconvenience of separation, saw that Liz was not prepared to relent. She had taken a long time to reach her decision, as with most things she did, and there was no changing her mind.

They agreed to part amicably, sell the house and split the proceeds once the mortgage had been repaid – though Liz had paid most of the instalments. They lived together, in separate rooms for the year it took to sell the house. George's secret hope of a reconciliation was not realised. Liz found a flat to rent but George, in his own world as ever, had made no arrangements at all.

For a month after the house was sold, while the new owners had not yet moved in, he used a spare set of keys to speak back in every night to sleep, until he found lodgings with a local friends. Within a few weeks, his dodgy dealings had raised enough cash for him to rent a flat of his own, in Grays.

Jazz dislikes ghosts

Life without Liz was unbearably lonely for George, even though he had no shortage of friends and acquaintances for company. But he was able to reclaim their cat, Jazz, from the local charity cattery and the company of this affectionate, funny and frisky feline helped him settle into the solo life.

Jazz kept George content for over sixteen years and the love of cats would stay with him, growing into a deep love for all animals that converted him to vegetarianism. It was a time when George was at his lowest ebb since the isolation of childhood, but the hours spent in reflection and self-examination were the ground in which the seeds of his psychic awakening were sown.

He saw a ghost while decorating his bedroom.

The figure of a lady sat on the edge of his bed, rocking a baby. She seemed agitated, seemed to be shouting at him for upsetting and waking her baby, although George could hear no sound. His clairaudience skills had not yet developed. He moved closer to the figure, unafraid and curious. The figure started to fade as he got closer, becoming translucent, but didn't disappear.

Thinking that he was overtired and imagining things, he completed his nightly routine and went to bed. But the figure was there again the following evening and many evenings after that. Although he still couldn't hear or communicate with the apparition, he told her he was happy to have her visit and even stay, so long as she didn't upset the cat.

Jazz was put off anyway, no longer sleeping in the bedroom warming George with furry purring. He also took to staying out all night sometimes, unusual behaviour for this particular moggy.

George eventually had to vacate the bedroom as well. He moved his bed to the sitting room when the ghost insisted on climbing on to his bed, lying on top of him, causing a feeling of heaviness, stifling and suffocating.

The ghost remained a secret shared only with Jazz, because George was concerned about his image and reputation. He didn't want to be seen as some kind of weirdo who was out of his mind. She never appeared before visitors, but remained with him in the flat until he left it.

Bad business

More discreetly than before, in an organised and businesslike manner, George carried on making his living from dealing drugs, set up by another of his shady mates. He was now savvy enough not to court the attention of the authorities by his old "give-it-large' attitude.

The same mate called George one night for a favour: to deliver a package for him. George refused at first but relented when his friend pleaded there was no one else he could use, just this once, and the delivery was crucial. His friend dropped off the package and told George the buyer would call him.

The call came, to deliver to a block of flats where the buyer lived. Cautious George wouldn't risk entering an unfamiliar building and arranged to meet in the estate car park. The buyer came for the package clad in his dressing gown, but forgot the cash for the buy back in his flat, so George was compelled to enter the apartment anyway. The buyer had all the appearance of a hardened heroin user, as did another man in the flat. He stayed chatting for a few minutes, answering their questions about what else he could procure for them.

He would learn later that both the "addicts" were plain clothes detectives and the entire conversation was covertly recorded. Careful as he had been to avoid attention, a favour for a friend had brought George right into the orbit of the drug squad. Nothing happened right away and George left to carry on his nefarious activities, even more blatantly than before.

Every night was party night at George's place, drinks and drugs with his cronies into the early hours. It was in the early hours, some six months after the encounter with the heroin "addicts," that the police knocked on his door.

It was roundup night, a massive planned operation involving police raids all over Essex to seize drugs and guns – and the people involved in selling them. George, just a bit player, had become ensnared in something much bigger than he could ever have imagined. It was April 5, 2005 and George was just short of fifty years old when he found himself at Harlow police station with ten complete strangers and his dodgy dealing friend. George's devil-may care bravado disappeared as he realised this was going to be a lot more serious than any of his earlier escapades.

Some of his fear was allayed when his duty lawyer was able to speak with the police and establish that George was being charged just with selling the three ounces of cocaine he had delivered to the covert cops six months earlier. His dodgy friend and an associate also managed to get themselves "separated" from the bigger and heavier gang. He was charged with possession of cocaine with intent to supply and refused bail, whisked off to Belmarsh Prison.

Belmarsh

A category A-C prison, with a secure AA unit within for the really hard cases, Belmarsh was a totally different proposition form Chelmsford and a universe away from Spring Hill. The entire atmosphere was replete with anxiety, caution, suspicion, no favours given or received. Even the prison staff moved in pairs or groups, avoiding any close contact or familiarity with the inmates.

Tough as it was, experience of Chelmsford helped George slip into the right routine and behaviour. Ordering canteen, looking for jobs, "sussing out" the unsafe inmates, all were familiar concerns to him.

He started off sharing a cell with three others who had been arrested with him; it helped not to be dumped with complete strangers. Locked up twenty-three hours a day for induction week was bearable, but the constant complaints of his companions about their predicament became tiresome. George accepted his confinement as his due, while the others simply moaned about their misfortune at being caught, endless "if only" conjectures denying any understanding of their own offences.

Association time was available after the first week, with the freedom to shower, play pool, make phone calls and George settled into a more comfortable confinement, with a more relaxed relationship even with the prison staff. It was also a time of feeling more settled inside himself, more accepting of his situation and his responsibility for his behaviour and predicament. Even though he was charged with a crime he had not committed – he was just delivering as a one-off favour, not actually selling – he took it as just desserts for the other offences that he had perpetrated daily, unnoticed and unpunished.

Knowing he was in for another prison term when he appeared in court, George got his nephew to terminate his tenancy of the flat and dispose of the effects, including the prized BMW from his lottery win. He was now completely adrift, with no ties to the world outside the walls. Liz visited regularly, but they were definitely no longer an "item."

Acceptance changed his conduct as well, no longer the cheeky, challenging bravado he had adopted all his life. It was a seminal change that would be key to the spiritual epiphany to come. No longer the restless maverick, George spent more time on reflection, realising that prison was the only way he could have stepped off the mad merry-go-round his life had become.

Reflection brought the realisation of his role and responsibility and real tears – remorse and regret at first, then joy at the fact that the nightmare could, finally, be nearing resolution. He began to write simple poems to record his rumination – about himself, his impact on others, the role of his parents in forming the personality he had played for so long. The resolve to reform began to grow and strengthen; he determined to discard his dissolute ways once he had served whatever sentence the court might impose this time.

The "new" George soon experienced the reward of his more mature behaviour – a job as "tea boy" came his way without having to wait weeks as he had in his previous prison term. He was given his own cell, but was out working from nine until six every day, including a two-hour lunch break.

As a trusted prisoner, he worked in the officers' rest room and had free run of the wing when he wasn't actually serving. He could make himself tea and toast anytime he pleased. Being trusted to keep the cupboard stocked was an important sign of his steady status; that the officers called him by his first name was another indicator that he was accepted as a responsible inmate. It did his credibility no harm when, finding an officer's cosh in the mess one day, he discreetly handed it in to the Hub office to avoid any trouble for the officer – or himself.

The gym at Belmarsh was George's next aspiration, but he faced problems with the security check. There were fears that, like the others with whom he was arrested, he might have a score to settle with one of the gang, a fellow who was suspected as being an informer for the police. The "grass" had been moved to another wing for safety, but all wings used the one gym.

One of the officers to whom he served tea told him that there were worries George might extract some form of vengeance on the suspected squealer. George explained that he was not part of the gang, laying out the circumstances of how he was involved in the roundup.

He was interviewed and awarded his prized position in the gym, with all the perks. He was now out of the cell seven days a week, including some evenings. He got to wear gym kit instead of the prison greys, eat and shower in the gym, use the gym laundry to wash his clothes, work on his own fitness. He applied himself assiduously and worked up to a supervisory position in the eighteen months he spent on remand.

Life at Belmarsh, in contrast to his previous stays in prison and even outside, was settled and safe, without any serious incident and barely any unsavoury incident.

Sentence stitch-up

It was in court that George discovered one disadvantage of having separated from the others who were arrested with him.

The two prisoners who had been 'separated' from the rest of the gang as smaller fish, had concocted a story that put George up as the ringleader of their trio, controlling the drugs and the cash. They had sold this story to the solicitor who represented all three of them and the solicitor had arranged for their cases to be considered before his. By the time it was his turn, on the fourth day of trial, his conviction in this role was all but certain; dismayed by the picture painted in court, George's new state of acceptance still prevailed. He deserved what he got, in his new frame of mind.

George received a sentence of four and a half years, less the eighteen months already spent on remand. It could have been a lot worse, he consoled himself, if he and the three others had not managed to separate himself from the main body of the gang. He hoped to return to Belmarsh and the cosy sinecure he had managed to achieve there, had left his kit there and been reassured by the officers that his job and his solo cell would be waiting for him.

It didn't work out that way, because prison officers can't control the intake. By the time he was sentenced, Belmarsh was full. George had to spend a night in a holding cell at Basildon Police Station with two complete strangers, devoid of even the bare comforts of prison. The next day, after a brief panic he might be sent to Birmingham and too far for Liz to visit, he was put on the bus to HMP Bullingdon in Oxfordshire – the county seemed to monopolise George's life behind bars!

Within a couple of days – without a smoke, because his "spends" had not yet been transferred to Bullingdon and his stuff was still at Belmarsh – the new, disciplined George secured a job in the prison laundry and settled into a new routine. Good behaviour and almost certainly good fortune followed the new, improved lawless Lawson, because within six weeks he was transferred to HMP Onley. The prison grapevine, conversation with other convicts and friendly screws, suggested that Onley was a good place to pass prison time.

Onley not lonely

A category B/C prison, Onley also included a Youth Offenders facility. Unusually, the cell doors in the reception wing were left open all day. There was no sense of the isolation and loneliness George felt behind a solid metal door, especially when the inspection flap was closed and he couldn't look out. The relief was real and palpable, even for a man used to being locked away.

He requested work in the gym, when asked what kind of work he would like to do at Onley. Not likely to happen, he was told. So he asked for a job in the kitchen, work with which he was well acquainted and which offered the perk of extra rations for his fitness regime.

He got the job, but was only in it for three days before an officer from the gym knocked on his cell door in the evening.

"You start work in the gym on Monday, Lawson," the officer informed George. "You must have friends in the right places."

One of the officers at Belmarsh had happened to be on a training course with another from Onley. Knowing that George had moved there, the Belmarsh officer had chatted to the Onley man and spoken well about George's conduct and attitude, recommending him as a steady man who knew his way about a gym.

He worked in the gym seven days a week, with some evenings, enjoying the same perks as gym work at Belmarsh – no prison garb, access to better food and laundry facilities. He earned the trust and support of the officers, who would spend time talking to him about his life and times, sorting out minor issues, encouraging him to study for and achieve a level two qualification as a gym instructor. A long-term prisoner, serving twelve years and familiar with the ways and means of Onley, became a fast friend and ally, easing the experience further.

The sense that life seemed to be taking him on a different course began to pervade George's perception and reinforce his determination to improve his mind, body, life. Unseen influences seemed to be at work, his good fortune seeming beyond mere coincidence.

The same sense guided him spontaneously to select a book on near-death experiences on his next visit to the library – he had been heading for the canteen, not even thinking of reading or books. Utterly entranced by what he learned about "the other side," he returned the next day to borrow two more books on the subject. As he completed this reading, he felt impelled to look further into the idea of life after life. He borrowed books about mediums next, biographies of Derek Akora and Gordon Smith, progressing to yet more books and audio tapes about mediums and mediumship.

All the mystic material mentioned the importance of meditation, so George began to practice making his mind still. One of the exercises he practised was putting cards face down on a table and trying to "read" them. He was gratified that his ability to predict correctly grew stronger with patient practice – and there was no shortage of time to do it! Meditation brought a feeling of warmth and comfort that George had never experienced before and this kept him keen to continue working at it.

Three months short of the end of his sentence, although comfortable enough in his confinement at Onley, he applied for category D status and requested transfer to an open prison when this was granted. It felt like the right thing to do, even with just twelve weeks left to serve.

Spectres at Stanford Hill

In May, 2007, George was transferred to Stanford Hill open prison on the Isle of Sheppey in Kent.

Disoriented at first, fate had fixed things for him and within two days he had been offered a gym job; word had come down the prison officer grapevine that the Lawson lad was worthy of trust. Within four weeks, he achieved the status of gym "number one," as he had at Onley.

He was encouraged again by the support of prison officers and acquired a swimming instructor's lifesaving qualification. Not bothered any more about finding work outside, George began to consider a career as a gym instructor when he had served his time.

Onley had been too far for Liz to visit and they had mostly stayed in touch over the telephone. Liz was almost his only contact with the

de and he treasured the care and concern, comforting despite
ement.

Sheppey was a lot closer, but George didn't want her associated
with the sad life he was suffering. There was a deep sense that he needed
to do this part of his "journey" – a feeling of predestination and a path,
the need to surrender his lifelong urge to control and follow where it led.
Consideration for Liz, absolutely absent when they were a couple, was
part of a developing empathy that came with recognising his own part in
every predicament.

He didn't make use of the freedom to visit home for whole weekends, either. He did not want to inflict any more uncertainty or pressure
on the lady who, though no longer an intimate, still meant more to him
than any other person in his life.

The meditation he had begun at Onley had occasionally produced directional thoughts. As he continued the practice in Stanford
Hill, he began to see visions. As before, he kept this to himself.

Liz's grandmother, Lily, appeared during one meditation. She approached him, stroked his eyes and began to speak. George couldn't hear
a thing, just her mouth moving.

"I can't hear you!" George exclaimed in frustration. Lily just
moved faster, a blur, still soundless, looking anxious and frustrated herself.
All he could sense was that something was wrong and she wanted him to
know.

This was a visit he couldn't keep to.himself. The next morning,
George called Liz to ask if everything was OK. She assured him everyone

was fine. She called the prison the very next day to pass on the news that George's Nan Wilson had passed away the previous day.

He declined the offer to attend her funeral in Scotland. His conviction of life after life was now firmly set and the old pragmatic George reasoned that Nan was already in spirit, unhindered by time and space; all he had to do was tell her from the core of his heart that he loved her and would miss her.

Sound and vision

The frustration of this encounter, like all the other soundless spectres before, spurred George. He began to deepen his meditation. with still mind, he focused conscious attention on sound. Slowly, he developed the ability to hear clearly every time he was gifted with a vision.

He began to see visions outside the quiet solitude of his cell. Walking around the exercise field one day with another inmate, George saw a woman walking beside his friend.

"Tell him I'm here," she said to George. "He wants to hear from me."

I can't tell him that! George thought. *He'll think I'm crazy!*

The lady was insistent. George sensed that she would not leave until he gave in to her demand.

"I don't know what's happening to me," he said to his prison pal. "I keep thinking I'm seeing things."

"You on drugs?" His friend responded, only half joking – half the prison was on drugs or medication.

"Of course not," said George. "I'm clean, been clean for months. I just saw a woman walking by your side."

He described the woman, who was now smiling.

"That's my mum!" His friend exclaimed.

"She just wants me to tell you that she is here with you."

Both the men were stunned by the incident. George was so stunned, he resolved not to tell anyone else about it and asked his mate to also keep it quiet. Credibility is important in a small community of men and he didn't want to be known as a crazy who talked to ghosts.

Until another vision, this time a prisoner who had hung himself. This spirit wanted George to pass on a message to another prisoner and again was not open to be denied. After some thought about how to broach the idea, George decided on simplicity and directness.

"Do you have a friend called Dennis?" He asked the prisoner for whom the message was meant.

"I *did* have a friend called Dennis," the recipient replied.

The connection validated, George decided it was safe to carry on with the communication.

"He wants you to know he's alright now." George conveyed.

"He hung himself, but he wants you to know that he is fine now."

His fellow prisoner melted into tears.

"He was my best mate!" He sobbed. "I've been tormented about him hanging himself, how unhappy he must have been. My best mate! And I couldn't help him get happy."

Another "happy customer," to coin a phrase, although mediumship is about as far from common commerce as one can go. George was genuinely moved by the comfort his visitations brought to troubled comrades-behind-bars. He began to feel better about his developing abilities, less hesitant about putting them to use for others' peace of mind.

Visions didn't always involve communicating with sentient energies. Strolling the Stanford grounds one day, George saw long tables decked out with bunting and laden with food and drink, people in uniform moving about. He mentioned this to the prison librarian, who was of course familiar with George's particular passion for the paranormal. He showed George a book with old photographs of Stanford Hill, when it was used as an army barracks during the Second World War. There were photographs also of the victory celebrations hosted at the site when the fighting finally finished.

Emotional entertainment

Out in town at weekends, sitting outside the pub, watching Saturday shoppers and strollers, George began to be aware of the emotional energies swirling around the people who passed. Passions were on parade as much as people: frustration, envy, joy, love, loss, fear, all seemed to surround them, a sizzling spectacle George enjoyed.

Until he was assaulted by a heavy, oppressive, fearful feeling, a sense of choking as one particular lady walked by. He had the strong sense of physical abuse by her husband, could almost co-experience her sadness, fear, despair. He could hardly approach a complete stranger and ask if her husband was beating her. He was deeply shaken by the experience, his inability to affect the situation, the depth of the despair. He could have resolved to stop it all right there – this spiritual consciousness was not all fun and laughter all the way, it seemed.

He dove back into the library instead, reading about famous mediums and how they had coped with the emotionally exhausting aspects of the work. No more sitting outside the pub until he had sorted this out!

Reading about how these credible, respectable and successful mediums had helped hundreds heal the hurt of losing loved ones, he now began to think about a life doing the same work. Watching Colin Fry on TV, reducing so many of his audience to tears of joy as he confirmed their loved ones were still around them, was a turning moment. George could completely connect with the emotional response of the recipient and he made up his mind.

Forget gym instruction. He would become a medium.

The medium

As he watched Colin Fry consoling and comforting his TV audience with convincing evidence of their loved ones still alive in spirit energy, George reverberated with the immense emotional energy through the screen.

He thought: This is what I am going to do. Immediately followed by doubt: What are you on about? That's not you, it's not what you do!

And other thoughts came bouncing back, not his own, unbidden: *You don't have choice about it. This is the work you will do.*

So, how would he do this?

Church chastisement

Apart from his reading and his odd experiences of sensing, seeing and hearing spirit energy, George had precious little knowledge or understanding of spiritualism. The closest he could get to anything spiritual was the Catholic faith in which he had been raised but never practised.

He could not have chosen a more hostile source for information about spiritualism, the very anathema of the Catholic creed. Spiritualism is the work of the devil and that is that.

The priest at the first Catholic Church he found ushered him straight back out of the door.

"We don't have anything to do with that devilry," he blurted. "Look in the *Yellow Pages* and sort it out yourself!"

George followed the advice, finding several Spiritualist churches in the directory and trying to contact all of them. Spiritualist churches don't have pastors or staff resident at all times and are only open during service times, but George didn't know that. The only listed number in the book (George had no access to the internet) was the official one on the church premises, where the phone was unattended most of the time George was trying to call.

Persistent in his pursuit, George sought out the prison's Protestant vicar, a lady who was the utter opposite of her Catholic counterpart. She listened attentively to his account, used a search engine on her computer to find details of the Spiritualist National Union (SNU). She was also able ferret out that the president of the SNU lived in Chelmsford, on the opposite bank of the Thames estuary from Sheppey and Stanford Hill.

The prison church telephoned the president, a man in his eighties, on George's behalf and offered to pay his expenses if he would visit Stanford Hill for a two-hour visit with George. Lunch and tea were also laid on for the visit, when George poured out all of his psychic experiences. The veteran spiritualist consulted a well-worn pocketbook, riffling through it and jotting on a spare scrap of paper.

"I want you to get to a church as soon as you get out," he said firmly. "This is your nearest one."

He offered to search out helpful books for George from his own personal collection, which he would bring to their next meeting. George was released the following week, after a prolonged bureaucratic bungle. He called the president, who offered to send a parcel of books to his home. George asked him instead to give him the titles of the books; he wanted to buy them himself, for his own library.

Home from home

Liz agreed to accommodate George when he was released, until he could sort out his own place to live. Her kindness created an air of calm comfort in her home, an ambience that George found immensely healing.

He avoided any contact with the crowd he used to favour, connected with like-minded people in the community now. He introduced himself to Grays Spiritualist Church, where he became a regular. He also attended ceremonies and workshops at other churches and centres nearby, notably Corringham. His commitment to the spiritual journey was complete and his progress steady, slow but sure.

Spiritualism – and he would say Spirit itself — provided George with a sense of community and of belonging, and the conviction that he was on the right and righteous path. He watched and learned how other mediums worked, confirming his faith and belief in life beyond life. He attended development circles, to improve his own practice.

Over the years and months, he gave countless readings and platform demonstrations, with impressive validation of accuracy. Extracts from his development journal in the next chapter shows the ups and downs of his journey, and attest his ability to "connect" with eternal energies. The people he encountered almost all helped and encouraged him, most notably Jackie Stevens, a successful medium for over thirty years.

George met Jackie at the funeral of Bill Bell, a venerable gentleman who hailed from Stoke on Trent and had helped to build the Church. Bill didn't attend the church except on the one night George was giving a platform demonstration – he still appears for George when he is having a difficult time!

"Come visit me," Jackie said. "I would like to work with you one-to-one."

Stella and the SAGB

Jackie, recently bereft of her husband, lived with two German Shepherd dogs and four ferrets. George and Jackie worked a platform demonstration together and it was after this that Jackie suggested George should consider applying to join the Spiritualist Association of Great Britain (SAGB).

Jackie and George braved the Autumn rain to visit the SAGB headquarters, in Belgrave Square (now based in its own building in Battersea). Although a long-term member of the Association, Jackie couldn't find anyone to speak to her other than the receptionist, who gave them an application form needing two testimonials.

Stella Blair, one of the stalwarts and driving forces at the SAGB, called George to attend an Open Circle, which he did. Clearly happy with George's abilities, Stella invited George to attend on 10 October, to give one reading and one platform demonstration. He did so, and two days later received Stella's invitation to join the foremost Spiritualist organisation in Britain.

Guiding spirits

Like most practising mediums, George has spirit guides to help him with his work. Like many, there are other guides from time to time, but his chief guides are Native American Indians.

The first to make an appearance, during meditation, manifested in black and white. George asked the vision to show himself more clearly and the guide asked George to visit a local shop that specialised in old prints and photographs. The next day, George spent almost two hours in the shop, rummaging through hundreds of pictures of Native American

Indians, without success. Just as he was leaving, disappointed, he spotted a picture on the wall by the door: it was the image he was looking for, in full glorious colour, with a deep red bandana.

This guide has never given George his name, but seems happy enough to be called Charlie. Charlie is George's "go to" guide, whose presence is guaranteed at every sitting and demonstration.

The second guide to appear – for just a millisecond that seemed like an age – was also a Native American Indian. He sported two feathers at the back of his head and was wrapped in a colourful blanket.

"Who are you?" George asked.

"In two weeks, someone will talk to you about me," the apparition advised.

Precisely two weeks later, during a development circle, knowing nothing about George's vision, one group member started talking about a book she had read, *Bury My Heart at Wounded Knee,* the story of the struggle by a chief Standing Bear to recover his people's lands from the Federal Government. George sought out a copy of the book at the local library and there, looking exactly as he had appeared to George, was a portrait of the legendary leader of the Ponca tribe.

In further meditations, both Indians appeared to George. On one occasion, they took him to the top of a high mountain. Charlie transformed into a wolf and Standing Bear, naturally, into a bear. George felt himself transformed into a fledgling eagle and both his guides shooed him off the maintain to fly free and exercise his wings.

Standing Bear rarely interacts with George, though the medium always senses his quiet presence. Charlie is always present, to help connect the loving energies that want to communicate through George.

Another regular visitor is Mickey, who only appears in George's flat, through the doorway into his lounge – George's cats love to lie just next to this "portal." The very first time he appeared, a dirty-faced Cockney boy with a classic cloth cap, he approached George to say: "Someone's mummy is coming to see you, Mr George!" Sure enough, the next day George found himself giving a private reading to comfort the mother of a young boy who had passed from physical in an accident. Mickey regularly connects George with the spirits of children

Development Journal

Keeping a journal is an essential element in the development of every medium. It serves as a reinforcer when motivation may be dipping and, often, may reveal insights on re-reading that might not have emerged immediately.

The following extracts have been kindly disclosed and shared by George to trace his progression and highlight significant events, with some editing for readability. The journal is full of uncountable readings, all validated by the subjects. Only entries that signify particular developmental moments have been included.

2007

I should have started this journal three or four months ago. Before I bring it up to date, I want to talk a little bit about how it started.

Nothing really stirred in me spiritually until my second term in prison. I had a clear sense that something was going on inside me. I was 49 years old. I had nothing outside those prison walls, no place to call home, no family. I don't think a day went by that I did not think about the wrongs I had done. I relived every moment. Seeing things from all sides really hurt. I didn't realise at the time, but I was being cleansed and guided. I couldn't forgive myself until later, when Spirit helped me to understand forgiveness.

(After release from prison) I went to my local Spiritualist Centre in Grays, Essex. Here it was that I learned my Spirit guide was a Native American. I knew this, of course. I knew what he looked like. This was validation for me. Another medium told me I had some gifts. I should either use them or let them go! There was no way I was going to let them go. They were gifts from the Divine Spirit. Everything was being put into place. It wasn't me organising all this.

I started going to workshops and was amazed at what came through. Over the past three months, I have developed quite well but am still a ways off being where I need to be, Many wonderful things have happened and much information has been given to me by spirit.

(At one Thursday circle) I was paired up with Alan. I gave him a message from his mother with good validation. I also had messages from his father and grandmother. He told me afterwards that he had been waiting a very long time for this, for his mother had died when he was nine years old. When wonderful messages like this happen, you get concerned that you have done everything properly, because they mean so much.

Monday, 5 November: I love spirit so much! I love having them around. I think about spirit an awful lot – when I am working, cooking, relaxing and even sleeping.

Tuesday, 6 November: (For a couple, man and woman.) I felt the presence of grandfather, soon interrupted by a practical joker, best friend of the man I was reading with Anne. I picked up on a nickname and reason for passing, I felt it. I also felt a great love for the couple from their friend.

(For a married lady with two small children.) The lady was concerned about her eight week old baby having stomach problems. Her uncle came through. I felt as though I had a bowel problems. She recognised who it was. I felt he was big, had tattoos but lost a lot of weight and hated hospital and his predicament. He kept showing me a boy more than twice. I told her the boy was about 10 years old. She said that was her uncle's son. I told her there was a picture of them both in the boy's bedroom. I described the picture and that it was not high up but about waist level. I also said his age when

passing was 35 years; I actually said 47 but was very quickly corrected by spirit to 35. What I loved about this was how the lady had come for something specific for herself and her child but that spirit had other plans. A message from your uncle! How wonderful!

I do love spirit and I do really want to do my best. I don't fully understand how I am doing this and it helps me to appreciate just how far I have to go. But I am in good hands.

Tuesday, 13 November: *What I can only describe as a fruitless evening. I only got a stepfather and his name, but that was it. I had to leave early as I was so tired, I slept for 15 hours that night.*

Saturday, 17 November: *(For Alan and at his home). I had already made a link with Alan's mum in the morning at Liz's flat. She told me she is with Alan every day. She made me feel very emotional. I could sense her love. She also gave me what sounded like Mary Rosslynn and Colleen. Alan told me his mum's name was Mary Carmen Jocelyn. I told Alan about the hospital his mother was in, three stories high, red brick with large white wooden framed windows. I told him about her father living out of town and working with animals (he was a blacksmith) and pictured his mum with a hat on and his father in uniform as a wedding picture. He showed me the picture at his home. She gave me the date 1947, which Adam confirmed was the year she died. She gave details of Alan's life, telling me he was a teddy boy, was in a scooter accident with a car, had a Cortina and spent a lot of money on a green car. (The car was actually grey.) She asked Alan to stop searching for her as she was with him every day. She also confirmed that he worked at Thames Board Mills and in the oil industry.*

Saturday, 24th December: *(A reading for Elana, who wanted to know if her ex-husband was dead or alive.) His parents came through first and I described them, giving memories of their time here. Her ex-husband showed himself in overalls. He told me about his social life, the split and where he went afterwards, all accurate. He also showed me or made me aware of an argument when a plate was thrown; also confirmed. I gave his eye colour, grey, that he was balding and with very large ears and a distinctive mouth as he got older. I told her he had a scar on his leg, supported Arsenal and was violent towards her. He was also sneaky, stealing things from the family home after he left. I have been concerned over this reading as it may have been I was picking up memories from Elana (who is also psychic).*

Sunday, 2 December: *(Reading for Pauline at her home.) I felt I had her father through. I spoke of his nature and his behaviour. I touched on his changing moods, arguments with his wife, heavy smoking. Pauline validated. I never really felt a strong connection but was able to give valuable information and memory links. I spoke of a motorbike accident, blindness in one eye and severe damage to his left hand side, a scar on his leg. All validated. Pauline agreed to check other facts and I will try another sitting to see if I can get a stronger link.*

Monday, 3 December: *(Monday night circle) We were asked without warning to do an address and a clairvoyant reading. I asked spirit for help and of course spirit duly supplied. I spoke about Christmas and how we should be aware of how easy it is to forget those who had very little. I thought it went quite well. I then told Jackie that there was chaos in her life at the moment and also a dispute in the family. It was not her doing. Instead of jumping in* *with both feet, I asked her to take two steps back and observe. It would be her who would resolve it. I felt I had her father. I gave her the name Colin; I realise now I should've just said "the letter 'C'?"because her father's name was actually Cecil. All the rest was accurate.*

Friday, 7 December: *(For a lady) I sensed young spirits around her. I gave her four or five names, all validated. I gave ages of those that passed young and the names of William or Bill, John and Cindy. She confirmed the first two and asked if the third name could be could be Candy instead of Cindy. I agreed that it was.*

Friday, 7 December: *Went to my spiritualist centre for some healing. I felt my energy is maybe low. After the healing, I told David that an elderly man wearing a cap, with two medals on his jacket was near him. I also mentioned an allotment. I said this man liked a Stout beer and worked in West Ham. I also told him that this man must've hurt his leg and had pain around the lungs. David confirmed he still had the two medals that his grandfather had won in the First World War as a stretcher bearer. He confirmed all the information, including the fall from a chair, hurting his leg and then contracting pneumonia from which he never recovered. God bless David and his grandfather.*

Monday, 10 December: *Today I want to write about my thoughts and feelings on the spiritual part of me. I still have very good days and some bad days. Those bad days are because I allow questions to enter my head. I feel it is healthy to question. I have such love for spiritualism and I feel this is somehow getting in the way of my life. It is very important to live your human life, as this gives the balance one needs. Spirit will never go away, so* *never fear that once they have seen your heart and are pleased with what they see, they will ever abandon you. They talk about you to others. They understand your thoughts, feelings and ambitions. The contract that you wrote before arriving on earth is known to them. As an individual I have reached a turning point, an inward turn and it is alien to me in so many ways. I love this turn because my soul understands. "This is who I am!" My soul screams to me. I am a messenger and feel glad and honoured to be given such a role. I feel great love for all those around me and that pleases me so much. To know, feel and understand love is such a gift. I have lived many lives to be where I am now and feel that the lessons and experiences are coming together in a way that was planned. I understand fully that I am so far off where I need to be, but it is an honour to be part of a grand plan. The inward realm is a beautiful place to be.*

Friday , 14 December: I am still doubting myself and I'm confused about where some of the information actually comes from. I am becoming very aware of the sadness in my world and have been moved to tears on a couple of occasions in the last couple of days. I feel I should be doing more spiritual work on my own development. I called Sandy and told her how I was feeling. She said I must shut down and be patient.

Saturday, 15 December: Went to Wickford to drop off presents for the children in a women's refuge. These were kindly dedicated by my circles. Whilst there, I was handed a letter from Nick Sinclair which said that I had been given honorary membership to the Knights Templar UK. I am very humble and grateful for this.

Thursday, 20 December: I went to Ramsgate as my nephew believed he had a ghost in his house and he was becoming concerned. I smudged every room and laid seaweed in each corner of each room. I did not feel anything bad, that they had been messing with any Ouija board and are both believers of the spirit world. I felt that they had opened themselves to spirit and spirit had been visiting. I asked the lost spirit to walk to the light as I smudged. (The journal entry includes details of readings for Nichola, Rosie's daughter and Ben, Nichola's boyfriend. For both of them, George gave validated details of their grandmothers.)

Sunday, 30 December: I have been dreaming quite a lot and have been very aware of activity around my flat. I am certain I am being prepared for something. There has been a smell around the flat. I thought something may be burning. I think it is a burning wood fire and it is one of my guides. I think it may be Merlin. The other evening, I was in bed and had different smells come to me: the burning wood fire, then lavender, then pipe tobacco and a sweet smell like pot pourri. I am hoping that all will be told to me soon.

2008

Saturday, 5 January: (One of three readings at Linford) I got the spirit of a man, reasonably young, who said his death was a tragedy (he was 40 years old and died of a heart attack, I learned later). I said I had a brotherly feeling about this man. He was a lady's brother-in-law. I saw a large man who loved his food, I saw motorbikes, large manual working hands, and a particular jacket he wore. All was confirmed to be correct. I spoke of headaches, depression and medication. I spoke of things going on in his head. He was, in fact, a schizophrenic on heavy medication. I passed on a message including thanks for two men who took care of all the arrangements for the funeral. All this was validated. I then began to wheeze and felt I had someone else step forward. I said it was her grandfather. She said it was and he had suffered from emphysema. I said he was a very quiet and gentle man wore glasses, also confirmed. I gave a memory about an accident on or by the fence. She told me that when she was little girl she threw a stone over her grandad's fence and hit the neighbour's little girl.

Sunday, 13 January: I went to the spiritualist centre and took up my position with some friends to watch the medium. Dave, the President of the centre, came to me and said that the medium had not turned up, would I help if needed? Before I could really think about it, I said yes. Before I knew it, I was on the platform with Dave and Joan, a bona fide medium. Dave and I did the opening address and I talked about my responsibility to the people I give readings. Spirit was already involved, because when I finished my address the congregation applauded. I went first and gave full readings straight off. I did labour with the first one but the father came through and helped me. I have to admit I was itching to get back up there and kept being drawn to one particular lady but as yet I had no link. (Eventually) Felt I had a link for the lady. I was drawn to give her some details of who was through, her mum and dad, and how proud they were of her. I then began to get information that was far too personal to include in my journal, but was confirmed by her.

Tuesday, 15 January: (Corringham circle) Ann allowed me to be lead medium. For the first lady, I had her grandfather. I described him and spoke about his mannerisms, gave cause of death. I also talked about hospital con-

ditions and how he would've worn an oxygen mask. I spoke about three people being at his bedside when passing on and also mentioned she passed at home with the daughter. She understood all of this. For the second lady I had several spirits coming through, all wanting to give her upliftment. I spoke to her about a man who was giving me pains, mainly on the top half of my body; I felt this was an accident. She told me it was a friend who had fallen off a roof. I also spoke of a beautiful child, had wonderful curly blond hair that made him look like a little girl. This was her stepbrother, who had died at the age of four. I gave her messages and also spoke about her split from her husband. She confirmed all of this.

Friday, 18 January: (Healing session at Grays) I spoke with Lou Lou about fears that seemed to have been installed in me since working the platform. She asked me if I'd spoken to spirit about them. So I did and everything was explained to me.

Monday, 28 January: (Monday circle, fledgeling night) I gave a message to little Dave, a wonderful healer at Grays. I have read Dave a couple of times before, given evidence and confirmation. I feel Dave was a safety net at first, because I was scared of failing. But the message this time was meant to go to him, because he needed to hear it. Fear must never be allowed to interfere with spiritual messages! I find this difficult to accept sometimes and I think I am my own worst enemy. Spirit are working with me, but my awareness is not what it should be. Truth, truth, truth is the only path. I gave a small reading to an unknown man. I was happy with it but it is not about how I felt. It is about how the sitter so comforted. I love spirits so much! Thank you, spirit and guidance.

The last couple of days I have felt distant and I feel I bring this on myself. I strive for so much, forget about who and where I am. I should never be discontented with the gifts of love, patience and compassion which are given to me. I am where I should be and I must begin to know this.

Tuesday, 29 January: *(one to ones with Ann Clarke) I didn't really feel connected in the two sittings. I was feeling and acting distant. I sometimes wonder if this is what I want to do. I feel that it's my spiritual journey which is important. I am confused, to tell the truth. people say lovely things to me. I find it hard to accept sometimes, as I do not wish to get caught up with ego! I am a messenger. Platform work is very difficult and it does affect me. I think this is because I am still so far off where I need to be??*

I must work harder. I know my heart and I am learning to know myself. That, in itself, is a journey worth taking.

Tuesday, 5 March: *I have been reading Estelle Roberts book, "50 Years A Medium." I am so impressed with this lady's dedication to her work as a spiritualist medium, healer and much, much more. She is a real inspiration to me. A truly remarkable lady, with wonderful gifts. If I could be just 25% as good as dedicated as her, I would be happy, but, may I add, still not satisfied and would strive to do better. I can only hope and pray that the divine spirit allows me to do this work in a similar way. God bless you, Estelle and Red Cloud. You have brought so much to this world.*

Wednesday, 13 February: *I am very happy on the path I have chosen. It fills me with so much that has been missing in my life for so long. I believe that my spiritual journey is so important to me and others I have not met yet. I know I have free will, but I am not sure if platform medium work is for me. I* *may well be at a bridge of chaos at the moment. I will ask my guides for help. I know the medium work I am doing is important. I can see that in my sitters' eyes. I guess that is the answer: it's not for me to see it is important, it is for the sitters. The trouble is I do see it is important. So much so, I want to be better. I want to really touch them, so they can truly believe that life goes on. I want to take away the pain. I want to live without fear of death.*

Thursday, 6 March: *There is a large gap in my journal. This is not because I have not done any spiritual work. It's for two reasons. Firstly I have been a bit lazy. More importantly, I do not want this to be true. We all love to have our egos stroked and I am no exception. I have, over the last two weeks, given around 15–20 readings. I have most certainly done work worthy of my journal, but I do not want to put myself on the back. What is important is that spirit have been so kind to me and help me without question.*

I have just finished reading "Red Cloud Speaks." I was deeply touched by what he had to say. I am beginning to understand more and more about myself, spiritualism and my world. I am so not worthy, but I am part of a whole. This is an honour. I really want to grow and grow and find my calling. I truly am not much of a man, but I'm trying. There are many wonderful things happening in our world that please me. I know I must work harder in order to find what I'm looking for, but I know I am close.

Wednesday, 19 March: *I am at a crossroads in my spiritual life. I have continued to do readings, either at circle in Corringham or at charity events. I am still receiving messages that are sometimes unbelievable, but I feel like I am struggling. I don't know what makes me feel that way. I feel, deep down, it may be fear — and fear is my biggest enemy. I am feeling like I don't want* *to do the mediumship work any more. Then an event comes up and I don't say "No!" And there I am, doing it. I love this works so much, so why should I stop it? I have not been very well lately, either. I need my guides to draw closer to me and guide me.*

Sunday, 30 March: *Have been very busy doing readings for charity and privately, as well as working at Corringham. I am pleased with the progress I am making. I do struggle with myself and it takes longer than I would like to actually realise where I am. It always is made clear to me in some way. I do not doubt my guides or spirit. It is myself I feel nervous about. I always get nervous before I do any spiritual development work or readings. Ann has told me this is spiritual energy. I must learn how to control it and use it to its full potential. I know she is right, but it does not stop me from feeling nervous. I get so scared sometimes, I feel like I want to get out of doing this stuff. Yet, every time the phone goes and I'm asked to do anything for work, I just seem to say "Yes." And these things always seem to work out well. I can't really explain it. There are definitely greater forces at work, so what can I do?*

Last Thursday at circle, I volunteered to be blindfolded. They put someone in front of me. First, I connected physically and discussed how that person was feeling. . Then, I connected spiritually to their grandparents. I gave evidence about them, which included what they look like, how grandma passed and little things like cooking and taking shoes off before coming in. At the end, I was able to say who it was in front of me. You do not need eyes to see what spirit wants to show you

Thursday, 3 April: *After a really good meditation, I felt very negative. I feel the circle is losing its true meaning. And it does not feel like there is enough* *love being shared by the group. Some people seem concerned only with them-selves. Jesus might have called it a brood of vipers, but he also would have been, and is, more forgiving than I feel at the moment. I pray for forgiveness for myself.*

Tuesday, 24 April: *It has been quite sometime since I have put my pen to this journal. Many wonderful things have happened. I have been working, doing some private readings, a psychic supper as well as working at Corring-ham. I always seem to get good validation and messages. I have been invited to attend a few functions, because people are beginning to trust what I am trying to do. There have also been some testing times. Three ladies have been saying that I was having affair with a leading member of the circle. This is definitely not true. I have to admit I laughed and was angry. I have been feeling some very negative feelings from these ladies for a few weeks. I now send my love to all of them, not to put myself in that righteous please, but because I want to send love instead of anger. I am trying to learn humility, which I believe is born out of love for others. There are so many different and wonderful lessons to be learnt in this beautiful earth. But I'm pleased to know I have a long way to go. Every step is an adventure and I'm equally pleased with how far I have come. I have to thank Dave Young, Linda Young and Ann Clarke for believing in me before I did. I also again thank my guides and the Divine Spirit.*

Friday, 2 May: *Every day is painful for me as I remember my past and all those I have affected. I have closed many doors in my material world. There are many who hate me, dislike me and think I am not worthy of anything and I would not say they are wrong, because that would make me judge-*

mental. I feel the pain of my past. It is there and will always be there. Each day I send out loving thoughts to all who I have affected, that is all I can do. But I also use all those bad things in a positive way. I know for whatever reason I did those things, no excuses, and they have brought me to where I am today. I am no longer in denial. I have taken responsibility. I have moved on and evolved spiritually. The past will always remind me of where I want to be now, not where I was. I fully understand why people may think what they do; in fact, I respect it. I understand how hard it must be for someone to look at me, for thinking: "Who does he think years? He is a criminal, why should he have any gifts from spirit?" Well, I have asked the same thing when I mistrusted in spirit. The simple fact is that gifts are given to us to be shared, not for us alone. I have always shared my gifts, always shown everyone love and praise them when they have done well. I have always spoken highly of them and refused to be drawn into disputes. I have reached out for all and asked for nothing in return. Who you see now is who I am now not who I was. I see you all through spiritual eyes, I hear you with spiritual ears. I feel all you feel, I hear what you do not say. I care not what you think of me. What matters is that I love all of you, yesterday, today and tomorrow. These words have come from my heart and I give thanks to my God for not abandoning me where others have.

Sunday, 22 June: *Over a month since I've written in this journal. I have been lazy and busy at the same time. I have a new flat and I've been trying to get it ready to move into. Going to circle and development core classes, private readings, fledgeling nights and some charity work for churches. I have done more than twenty readings. I am full of wonder at what I get from spirit. I've* *had a most wonderful meditation, so real I could've reached out and touched when I was seeing. Vibrant colours, very clear images.*

Thursday, 30 August: *It has been so long since I have written anything in this journal. So much has happened. So many wonderful moments that really should be recorded. So much evidence I have not recorded. I'm afraid of becoming an egotist, ut I guess as long as that fear lasts it will not happen. I've been doing platform work — yes, the sort of work I said I would stop do-ing! Spirit have other plans and I am glad of it. I am working on my own at times but also with Ann Clarke and Sandy Wilkinson. It is lovely that they allowed me to work with them. I also visit Bill Bell, a lifelong spiritualist, who is 88 years old and a massive inspiration to me. I have to say that he is a special man. He will have a wonderful home in the spirit realm.*

Tuesday, 30 December: *I have been on a 10-day meditation retreat in Hereford. No talking or communication allowed. I enjoyed it, although it was hard at times, 6–8 hours a day meditating, but I feel it was worth it! December has been quite a hard month for me personally. I have by nature an addictive gene. I have abused alcohol this month. I feared for the links and contacts I have made in spirit. And of course for my own personal health and spiritual responsibility to myself. I've decided to stop alcohol for a long period, if not for good. Already, I feel better and stronger. I have not drunk for over a week. I do yearn for a drink and a smoke, but I haven't caved in yet!*

2009

Friday, 6 February: I have been very busy since Christmas. I have around 40 bookings for different centres this year. It is my first year on my own. Circle has started and I have been active with that. Bill Bell, my dear friend, and Joe Smith are both not very well. Both are 80 years of age. They are both lovely men. I am particularly close to Bill, he really inspires me – such a happy man, who loves his spiritual life. You cannot fail to feel happy in his presence. I have learnt so much from him. His understanding is beautiful. I often see his smile in my minds eye. God bless him and God bless Joe. So many wonderful events that happened because of spirit: wonderful proof, wonderful messages. My human feelings and my mind still interfere and I wonder if this is real. I am working hard to overcome my thoughts. I have so much to be grateful for! Just look at me now: no crime, not so selfish, independent, no smoking, no drinking, going to the gym and working for spirit. Ann, Jean, Paul and I have started a new circle. Have a really good feeling about it.

I have been staying with Liz for about a week because of the snow. It is very cold over in my flat! Liz is very kind to me and I love her very much. We laugh a lot together. I am trying to get my mind, body and soul in good condition. Food is really the new addiction in my life and I'm trying to control that by going to the gym and watching what I eat — so hard!

Walk quietly on this earth, be happy and comfort all in need. Be good to yourself. Nurture all that has been given to you by God. Be thoughtful of others and try to understand what has been shown to you. All you are is within you. Know that you are loved beyond words. Amen.

Tuesday, 8 June: I had a dream that my brother Frank came to me. That being missing (only in the dream, as he is well and at home in Ockendon). I knew he was in spirit but he never knew it was a rescue. He had been murdered by a Frenchman called Marion Marroonii or Marrinoo, viciously beaten around the head. It may be a symbolic dream, I don't know. My brother denied that he had passed (in the dream). I told him a few things and asked some questions. He then realised, saw friends and family and moved on. It was emotional. I may have rescued a person who may have looked like my brother.

Sunday, 28 June: I asked Liz not to go to the Orsett boot sale. There is a blindspot on the road when leaving there and getting back on the road. I thought something was going to happen and I was worried she would be involved. She said she was going, but would be careful. She called later to say she got held up by a neighbour talking for 20 minutes and when she arrived at Orsett, firemen were cutting two girls out of the car at the blackspot I had mentioned.

2010

Friday, 10 January: I have not written in my journal for so long, I think it is due to laziness on my part. Have continued to work for spirit and the proof and evidence just keeps on coming. I have been busy in 2009 and will be busier in 2010. I have also been talking on the Mayan prophecies for 2012. I spoke at Harlow and will be speaking at St. Celia's in March this year. I feel I had struggled in 2009 and the beginning of 2010. This is in a physical way. I have been ill quite a lot, including vomiting and tiredness. I've been a vegetarian for awhile now, so I think the change in my diet has something to do with it. The other part is my drinking too much. I'm trying to address this issue. I have also put on a lot of weight, which does upset me, but I must not allow it to wear me down. I'm looking forward to working in 2010. I have worked at Wickford and Grace Church. Both are wonderful. Spirit come forward with very good evidence: dates, names, places. Thank you so much, spirit for allowing me to do this work.

Wednesday, 17 February: *I have been very busy with service and private work. There is always good evidence given by spirit. There is also a lot going on around me. I believe I have a new guide, an aborigine called Joseph. I have seen him in meditation and when waking, in my mind's eye. I have had many wonderful dreams, flying, levitating and have seen the world from a distance. I have travelled through space, I have seen spaceships and creatures we might be afraid of that are in fact very kind. I have seen the brightest of lights. I saw a baby in a space suit. I've passed through ceilings and felt the vibrations as I passed. I am searching to be a better person, to get closer to who I truly am. I have found myself questioning others' motives. I seem to understand or see hidden agendas in others. I must begin to understand this, as it has value in that it can help??*

Sunday, 25 July: *It has been three months since I have written in this journal. I still have issues with alcohol and weight. I have been working continuously for spirit. One of the hardest things is detaching from ego. It is nice when you are told you are good, but you have to let that go very quickly as it is not you but spirit working through you — if we allow them to do their work, because it hinders if we get involved. I am once again going to try and address my weight and drinking. I have also been given an opportunity to* *audition at the SAGB in Belgrave Square, London. I have been working a lot over the past three months. Spirit watch over me and take care of me. Thank you so much, spirit.*

Thursday, 7 October: *Had a very busy month since I last wrote in here. I have worked many churches and had a lot of private sittings. There has been some wonderful evidence given. I have an audition at the SAGB on Sunday. I'm going to write in this book more often. I have over the past few months been giving messages about people involved in stabbing, with some remarkable evidence.*

Sunday, 10 October: *I had my audition at SAGB this week. I had to give a one half hour private reading and a one hour demonstration on clairvoyance. I received a phone call the next day. They were very pleased with the work spirit did through me and I will soon be working for them at the headquarters in Belgrave Square.*

2011

Thursday, 17 March: *I have been working at the SAGB for several months now. It has been a great learning curve for me. I have given, through spirit, some of the most wonderful evidence and have had the privilege of working for spirit to help so many people. This is the most wonderful journey of self discovery, to realise my part in this world. I think about this work every day, all day.*

Personal perspectives

George's song

BEHIND ME

I was born a Taurean, what can I say,

six-pounds-eight on the nineteenth of May.

I remember my life since before I was two,

fifty-six years – it seems time just flew.

> *I remember my brothers and the times that we had,*
>
> *most were not good, but all were not bad.*
>
> *I prayed so hard for things to be right,*
>
> *I prayed for my mum and dad not to fight.*

I remember my school days, they went by so fast,

the friends that I made are the friends of the past.

I remember my anger, my joy and my pain,

I remember not being a family again.

> *I remember living a life that was so fake,*
>
> *if there was anything I needed – I simply would take.*
>
> *I remember my manhood with so many scars,*
>
> *I remember my sadness just looking through bars.*

I remember my joy when I fell from grace,

and my life's journey was gathering pace.

I saw my life from every angle,

this complicated person began to untangle.

> *I discovered myself, I learnt how to love,*
>
> *with divine intervention and guides from above.*
>
> *My prayers had been answered; I am truly your friend,*
>
> *this battered old life is well on the mend,*

Message from Mumbai

My husband started visiting SAGB in early 2002 as an inquisitive visitor based on the recommendation of a senior office colleague/close family friend. Trips used to be two to three times a year. Coming from India on work related matter to London and taking out a 30-minute time slot for a sitting session with a medium is all that he planned for and look forward to.

The first few sessions were a revelation to us about after life and how spirits are around us and the ways and the extent to which they go to describe their existence by talking about past incidences, places and matters of love and concern – strengthening our belief on the link between life on earth and the spirit world. It also started cementing our faith and trust on mediums and mediumship.

In December 2004, we lost our son and were completely devastated. Between Jan 2005 and March 2010, we visited SAGB quite a few times and definitely on my son's birthday. My husband got work in London and we lived there for a few months and then we moved to New York and then in early 2007 we returned back to Mumbai, India. During this traveling period and subsequently also on my son's birthday in March of each year me and my husband used to just travel for a day to do one session at SAGB and communicate with our son and wish him happy birthday and a good life in the spirit world. It was a very emotional and tearful journey for both of us but worth every minute once we were in the sitting session.

George came into our lives in March 2012 when we first met him for a sitting. By that time, we had adapted ourselves to arrive in London on an early March winter morning after a 10-hour non-stop flight from

Mumbai, shower/change/breakfast at Heathrow airport followed by a tube ride to Belgravia Square for our sitting session around noon. When we met George and he put on the cassette recorder on start, we were already tearful in anticipation of communicating with our son.

George came straight to the point saying that there is a young boy standing between us and his hands are on our shoulders. He is smiling, bubbling with joy and identifying us as his parents. And from thereon, George started sharing with us, about evidences that he is indeed our son – things about his medical history, under what circumstances he passed away, the location, the time of the day, how old is he today, what he likes, places he loves to visit, his favorite toys, books, teachers, relatives – the whole nine yards. It was like our son standing in front of us and speaking out a summary of everything that has touched his life since he could re-member.

It was one of our most fascinating and life-changing sitting ses-sion at SAGB. On our return journey to India, our analytical side of the brain was trying to decipher if we are under a hypnotic spell of George who was controlling and reading our mind or was it truly an out-of-world experience. We just could not fathom as to how can someone be so accur-ate. Like for example, our son mentioned that his favorite toy is Spiderm-an and Noddy – which is true as he use to eat, pray, walk, play, sleep with these toys. But then he tells George that – "......tell my papa that he should not keep these soft toys in his cupboard behind the suits. It covers the toys and they need air to breathe. He should take them out and keep it above his brother's section of the toy cupboard where it will be easily visible........". This statement stunned us since it was accurate to the T. My husband had kept both the soft toys in his suit section at the back side behind the suits. George said that our son is saying all this to convince his parents that he is always there at home with us and never left us – except he is no more in the physical form, but in the spirit form.

The next few months we talked at length about this session and agreed that for the next session scheduled for March 2013, we should request SAGB to give us George as our medium. Until this point in our life since we started our visit to SAGB in 2002, we had never asked for a specific medium but were lucky to have quite a few times the same medium – but never a requirement or request from our side. But for the forthcoming trip of March 2013, it was different – we really wanted to meet only George and through him communicate with our son in the spirit world.

We again met George in March 2013 but this time we could not meet him at SAGB as it was not his scheduled visit day. So, we called him to our hotel room near the airport for a private sitting. It was our son's birthday and we just did not want to miss the opportunity of knowing about his well-being and for wishing him. It was another wonderful sitting session – although emotionally tearful for us as parents, but the messages that our son gave through George was outstanding.

Our son spoke about how I miss him and what exactly I do when i feel like crying in his memory. He spoke about us changing the lock of our bathroom which was broken, fixing the wattage of the lights in the living room, telling his mom to take care of his younger brother's study and his younger sister's sibling fight over toys with his younger brother. He spoke about his father's most recent travel to New York and the Hershey chocolates he got for the family and where exactly is an extra pack of those chocolates hidden by his father for a rainy day. All true and accurate. It's like somebody is living with us in our house 24x7 but just not visible.

Towards the end of this session, our son said to George that – ".... tell my mom not to take so much pain to travel all the way to London just for this one session, that he is always with and around her.......". This moved me so much that I kept on crying. We were almost to the end of our session and that's when George asked if we had any questions to ask and we said that all our questions, fear about his well-being, concerns have been answered. Then George took our permission to ask one question and we said go ahead. So, he asked where do we come from and why was our son talking about the pain of travel. We then shared our 10-hour flight each way ordeal from Mumbai to London and back to Mumbai and then spend the day walking around the streets of London just for this one hour sitting session at the SAGB. George appreciated the situation and suggested that at any point if we are sad and depressed we should drop him an email and he will pray for us. He further suggested that we should think about - instead of the two of us coming to London just for a day, he can come to Mumbai and not just spend an hour of sitting session but a few days. And if there are other like-minded people who believe in the spirit world and would like to have a session then he would be happy to conduct those sittings. We heard him and mentioned that we will think over it.

In the following months, me and my husband revisited this year's session conversation topics and it further reinforced George's ability as a very high level medium, his clarity of what he sees and the way he communicates the message to us. We also spend a good deal of our time pondering over our son's message to me for not to take the travel pain and George volunteering to come to Mumbai. A lot questions about – is it the right way to do it, are we commercializing George's plan just to circumvent our cost and travel issues, or is there a larger plan that the spirits are guiding us to. We could not find any answers so we left the issue open until we meet George again in March 2015.

In our next session at SAGB in March 2015, we had more pleasant surprises with the disclosures that our son shared with us. He spoke about the recent events, birthdays, the color of dresses that we wore on our anniversary, about our forthcoming holidays in May – each of them to a level of clarity that only someone who had participated in the event/planning would have known. By now, our love and eagerness to know about our son and his stories of involvement in our day to day lives through the spirit world was intriguing as well as fascinating. Interestingly, he also knew that we were coming to London for a week-long holiday towards the end of the Indian summer (end May/early June 2015) and he looked forward to seeing us then. Our last question to him was if he will be happy and continue to come and meet us if instead of we coming to SAGB London, we request George to come to Mumbai for a few days. His response was positive and encouraging as he wanted to show George his drawer where his mom had kept his clay footprint. This was again a very positive support to confirm that George was a genuine medium and connecting the both worlds in an honest and faithful way for the souls to meet and heal.

Come May/June 2015 and we were London, but this time with my son's younger brother and sister. We all called George to our apartment at High Street Kensington and for the first time my two kids in this world met George and sat through a part of the private session where they asked naïve but intelligent questions to George about his relationship with their brother in the spirit world and how will they know if it is the truth or fiction. George then related them stories about significant instances in the recent past – their birthday cake type, color of shirt, favorite toy, recent holiday games that they played and enjoyed. My children had an expression of utter disbelief as to how surreal this was. Then my son in the spirit world also shared an incidence each with his siblings as to how during an exam time/game time he was there helping them. He lastly, gave them a message that he will always be around them and they should rely and call on him for any help or support they need emotionally and spiritually.

Post this, we were now in the affirmative that we should bring George to India for March 2016 and we did that. My husband made arrangements for his visa, tickets and his stay at an apartment where my husband's ex-boss stayed. This was the same gentlemen who introduced us to SAGB in 2002 not knowing that it was destiny's design of preparing us for grief management and counselling at the hands of George. We also arranged for 8-10 private sitting sessions with some of our friends and each of them were in shock and awe as to the accuracy of George's reading and communication of the messages from their near and dear ones in the spirit world.

This trip was followed by another three trips of George to Mumbai – in March 2017, Feb/Mar 2018 and then in June/July 2018 around the time of the FIFA 2018. In the March 2017 and 2018 trips we had arrangement for stay and private sessions of George at our club house and in the most recent Jun/July 2018 trip George stayed with us at our residence for 5 weeks. This was his private trip only for us and for his own private "meditation" time.

In summary, we think George is a very evolved spirit at a level far higher than us worldly mortals. He has a gift of clear listening and communicating in verbatim with no salt and pepper added to it. Listening and talking to him feels like we have a blessed life and the sadness of losing our dear son just dissipates away. His spiritual guidance strengthens our belief that spirits do exist, that they never leave you, that they care and protect you and whatever happens – it was destined to happen and it happens for a cause. Accept the cause, do good deeds, be humble, show mercy and gratitude and move towards salvation is what we have learnt in the last few years of knowing George.

We pray that his teachings and his sittings benefit all and he keeps growing and evolving as destined.

With Best wishes,

Reenaa A Singh
September 09, 2018
Mumbai, India

Testimonial from Grays

In my mind George has come a long way to understanding True Spirituality, the title he has given this book epitomises how we are all in the dark until we finally, to coin a phrase " finally see the light" which is in all of us.

Having known George for many years, he was in the darkness with his life choices, until he felt there had to be a better way of life, with this thought in mind He came to our Church, where even though we knew of George's past didn't stop us from making him welcome, there was no thought about it, we just did it.

George became very interested in the Spirituality that we taught, about life in the Spirit world, but more importantly about life on Earth. George became a member of our Spiritualist Circle, where he was guided to Meditate and allow thoughts that were not his own to come through, this in time George discovered he could communicate with those in the Spirit world, he felt the love that they gave, but also he could ease the suffering of the many people that grieve the loss of a loved one here in this life, He has worked tirelessly with, as he calls it "his Quest in life". George has researched many different Religions and Doctrine, finding that they are all borne from love which is True Spirituality, to help your fellow man.

George continues to serve our Church and also many other places of worship, and he is still striving to find the good in all people.

It is my pleasure to know George as he continues his Spiritual life and wish him well on his next endeavour

Dave Young

President

Grays Spiritualist Church

Everything happens for a reason.

There are no coincidences. What goes around, comes around. You need dark to see light.

Pithy phrases persist because they reflect constant truths. George's journey would affirm many of them. Certainly, his reflections on his own life confirm those above. From the horrors of home as a child, through the reckless wreck of of his life before Onley and Stanford Hill, everything now seems to have a sense of pre-ordination, essential steps in evolution.

The extreme ups and downs, the enormous variety of people and events he experienced also allowed him better to understand the immense diversity of the human condition.

"It's a crying shame to me that I had to go through three terms of being locked away before I got started," George says regretfully. "But without them I would still be the cocky control freak causing mayhem in people's lives.

"My life had to be stripped bare, down to nothing, before I could start building a better one."

Anger and blame, defiance and disobedience, all had to be eliminated before acceptance brought inner peace. The pain of prison was payback for the pain he had dished out, directly to those close to him, indirectly to those who depended on the drugs he dealt.

"The truth shall set you free!" George quotes the Christian promise with a wry smile. Facing the truth and remaining determined forever to deal only in honesty and the truth, are at the very core of George's spiritual faith.

The other prime principle for George today is service: a devotion to help others and bring comfort and joy wherever he can.

"Helping others is really also helping yourself," George claims.

"You become known as a friendly and helpful person. Making others happy means you are surrounded by happy people, enjoying the positive energy and being uplifted."

"It's what I was meant to do," George says. "So it's what I do."

Not the end.